Psychological Types

C. G. Jung

GENERAL DESCRIPTION OF THE TYPES

A. INTRODUCTION

In the following pages I shall attempt a general description of the types, and my first concern must be with the two general types I have termed introverted and extraverted. But, in addition, I shall also try to give a certain characterization of those special types whose particularity is due to the fact that his most differentiated function plays the principal role in an individual's adaptation or orientation to life. The former I would term *general attitude types,* since they are distinguished by the direction of general interest or libido movement, while the latter I would call *functiontypes*.

The general-attitude types, as I have pointed out more than once, are differentiated by their particular attitude to the object. The introvert's attitude to the object is an abstracting one; at bottom, he is always facing the problem of how libido can be withdrawn from the object, as though an attempted ascendancy on. the part of the object had to be continually frustrated. The extravert, on the contrary, maintains a positive relation to the object. To such an extent does he affirm its importance that his subjective attitude is continually being orientated by, and related to the object. An fond, the object can never have sufficient value; for him, therefore, its importance must always be paramount.

The two types are so essentially different, presenting so striking a contrast, that their existence, even to the uninitiated in psychological matters becomes an obvious fact, when once attention has been drawn to it. Who does not know those taciturn, impenetrable, often shy natures, who form such a vivid contrast to these other open, sociable, serene maybe, or at least friendly and accessible characters, who are on good terms with all the world, or, even when disagreeing with it, still hold a relation to it by which they and it are mutually affected.

Naturally, at first, one is inclined to regard such differences as mere individual idiosyncrasies. But anyone with the opportunity of gaining a fundamental knowledge of many men will soon discover that such a far-reaching contrast does not merely concern the individual case, but is a question of typical attitudes, with a universality far greater than a limited psychological experience would at first assume. In reality, as the preceding chapters will have shown, it is a question of a fundamental opposition; at times clear and at times obscure, but always emerging whenever we are dealing with individuals whose personality is in any way pronounced. Such men are found not only among the educated classes, but in every rank of society; with equal distinctness, therefore, our types can be demonstrated among labourers and peasants as among the most differentiated members of a nation. Furthermore, these types over-ride the distinctions of sex, since one finds the same contrasts amongst women of all classes. Such a universal distribution could hardly arise at the instigation of consciousness, ie. as the result of a conscious and deliberate choice of attitude. If this were the case, a definite level of society, linked together by a similar education and environment and, therefore, correspondingly localized, would surely have a majority representation of such an attitude. But the actual facts are just the reverse, for the types have, apparently, quite a random distribution. In the same family one child is introverted, and another extraverted.

Since, in the light of these facts, the attitude-type regarded as a general phenomenon having an apparent random distribution, can be no affair of conscious judgment or intention, its existence must be due to some unconscious instinctive cause. The contrast of types, therefore, as a, universal psychological. phenomenon, must in some way or other have its biological precursor.

The relation between subject and object, considered biologically, is always a *relation of adaptation,* since every relation between subject and object presupposes mutually modifying effects from either side. These modifications constitute the adaptation. The typical attitudes to the object, therefore, are adaptation processes. Nature knows two fundamentally different ways of adaptation, which determine the further existence of the living organism the one is by increased fertility, accompanied by a relatively small degree of defensive power and individual conservation; the other is by individual equipment of manifold means of self-protection, coupled with a relatively insignificant fertility. This biological contrast seems not merely to be the analogue, but also the general foundation of our two psychological modes of adaptation, At this point a mere general indication must suffice; on the one hand, I need only point to the peculiarity of the extravert, which constantly urges him to spend and propagate himself in every way, and, on the other, to the tendency of the introvert to defend himself against external claims, to conserve himself from any expenditure of energy directly related to the object, thus consolidating for himself the most secure and impregnable position.

Blake's intuition did not err when he described the two forms as the "prolific" and the "devouring" As is shown by the general biological example, both forms are current and successful after their kind ; this is equally true of the typical attitudes. What the one brings about by a multiplicity of relations, the other gains by monopoly.

The fact that often in their earliest years children display an unmistakable typical attitude forces us to assume that it cannot possibly be the struggle for existence, as it is generally understood, which constitutes the compelling factor in favour of a definite attitude. We might, however, demur, and indeed with cogency, that even the tiny infant, the very babe at the breast, has already an unconscious psychological adaptation to perform, inasmuch as the special character of the maternal influence leads to specific reactions in the child. This argument, though appealing to incontestable facts, has none the less to yield before the equally unarguable fact that two children of the same mother may at a very early age exhibit opposite types, without the smallest accompanying change in the attitude of the mother. Although nothing would induce me to underestimate the well-nigh incalculable importance of parental influence, this experience compels me to conclude that the decisive factor must be looked for in the disposition of the child.

The fact that, in spite of the greatest possible similarity of external conditions, one child will assume this type while another that, must, of course, in the last resort he ascribed to individual disposition. Naturally in saying this I only refer to those cases which occur under normal conditions. Under abnormal conditions, *i.e.* when there is an extreme and, therefore, abnormal attitude in the mother, the children can also be coerced into a relatively similar attitude; but this entails a violation of their individual disposition, which quite possibly would have assumed another type if no abnormal and disturbing external influence had intervened. As a rule, whenever such a falsification of type takes place as a result of external influence, the individual becomes neurotic later, and a cur can successfully be sought only in a development of that attitude which corresponds with the individual's natural way.

As regards the particular disposition, I know not what to say, except that there are clearly individuals who have either a greater readiness and capacity for one way, or for whom it is more congenial to adapt to that way rather than the other. In the last analysis it may well be that physiological causes, inaccessible to our knowledge, play a part in this. That this may be the case seems to me not improbable, in view of one's experience that a reversal of type often proves exceedingly harmful to the physiological well-being of the organism, often provoking an acute state of exhaustion.

B. The Extraverted Type

In our descriptions of this and the following type it will be necessary, in the interest of lucid and comprehensive presentation, to discriminate between the conscious and unconscious psychology.

Let us first lend our minds to a description of the *phenomena of consciousness.*

(1) THE GENERAL ATTITUDE OF CONSCIOUSNESS

Everyone is, admittedly, orientated by the data with which the outer world provides him ; yet we see that this may be the case in a way that is only relatively decisive. Because it is cold out of doors, one man is persuaded to wear his overcoat, another from a desire to become hardened finds this unnecessary; one man admires the new tenor because all the world admires him, another withholds his approbation not because he dislikes him but because in his view the subject of general admiration is not thereby proved to be admirable; one submits to a given state of affairs because his experience argues nothing else to be possible, another is convinced that, although it has repeated itself a thousand times in the same way, the thousand and first will be different. The former is orientated by the objective data; the latter reserves a view, which is, as it were, interposed between himself and the objective fact. Now, when the orientation to the object and to objective facts is so predominant that the most frequent and essential decisions and actions are determined, not by subjective values but by objective relations, one speaks of an extraverted attitude. When this is habitual, one speaks of an extraverted type. If a man so thinks, feels, and acts, in a word so *lives,* as to correspond *directly* with objective conditions and their claims, whether in a good sense or ill, he is extraverted. His life makes it perfectly clear that it is the objective rather than the subjective value which plays the greater role as the determining factor of his consciousness. He naturally has subjective values, but their determining power has less importance than the external objective conditions. Never, therefore, does he expect to find any absolute factors in his own inner life, since the only ones he knows are outside himself. Epimetheus-like, his inner life succumbs to the external necessity, not of course without a struggle; which, however, always ends in favour of the objective determinant. His entire consciousness looks outwards to the world, because the important and decisive determination always comes to him from without. But it comes to him from without, only because that is where he expects it. All the distinguishing characteristics of his psychology, in so far as they do not arise from the priority of one definite psychological function or from individual peculiarities, have their origin in this basic attitude. *Interest* and *attention* follow objective happenings and, primarily, those of the immediate environment. Not only persons, but things, seize and rivet his interest. His *actions,* therefore, are also governed by the influence of persons and things. They are directly related to objective data and determinations, and are, as it were, exhaustively explainable on these grounds. Extraverted action is recognizably related to objective conditions. In so far it is not purely reactive to environmental stimuli, it character is constantly applicable to the actual circumstances, and it finds adequate and appropriate play within the limits of the objective situation. It has no serious tendency to transcend these bounds. The same holdsgood for interest: objective occurrences have a well-nigh inexhaustible charm, so that in the normal course the extravert's interest makes no other claims.

The moral laws which govern his action coincide with the corresponding claims of society, *i.e.* with the generally valid moral view-point. If the generally valid view were different, the subjective moral guiding line would also be different, without the general psychological habitus being in any way changed. It might almost seem, although it, is by no means the case, that this rigid determination by objective factors would involve an altogether ideal and complete adaptation to general conditions of life. An *accommodation* to objective data, such as we have described, must, of course, seem a complete adaptation to the extraverted view, since from this standpoint no other criterion exists. But from a higher point of view, it is by no means granted that the standpoint of objectively given, facts is the normal one under all circumstances. Objective conditions may be either temporarily or locally abnormal. An individual who is accommodated to such con certainly conforms to the abnormal style of his surroundings, but, in relation to the universally valid laws of life. He is, in common with his milieu, in an abnormal position. The individual may, however, thrive in such surroundings but only to the point when he, together with his whole milieu, is destroyed for transgressing the universal laws of life. He must inevitably participate in this downfall with the same completeness as he was previously adjusted to the objectively valid situation. He is adjusted, but not adapted, since adaptation demands more than a mere frictionless participation in the momentary conditions of the immediate environment. (Once more I would point to Spitteler's Epimetheus). Adaptation demands an observance of laws far more universal in their application than purely local and temporary conditions. Mere adjustment is the limitation of the normal extraverted type. On the one hand, the extravert owes his normality to his ability to fit into existing conditions with relative ease. He naturally pretends to nothing more than the satisfaction of existing objective possibilities, applying himself, for instance, to the calling which offers sound prospective possibilities in the actual situation in time and place. He tries to do or to make just what his milieu momentarily needs and expects from him, and abstains from every innovation that is not entirely obvious, or that in any way exceeds the expectation of those around him. But on the other hand, his normality must also depend essentially upon whether the extravert takes into account the actuality of his subjective needs and requirements; and this is just his weak point, for the tendency of his type has such a strong outward direction that even the most obvious of all subjective facts, namely the condition of his own body, may quite easily receive inadequate consideration. The body is not sufficiently objective or 'external,' so that the satisfaction of simple elementary requirements which are indispensable to physical well-being are no longer given their place. The body accordingly suffers, to say nothing of the soul. Although, as a rule, the extravert takes small note of this latter circumstance, his intimate domestic circle perceives it all the more keenly. His loss of equilibrium is perceived by himself only when abnormal bodily sensations make themselves felt.

These tangible facts he cannot ignore. It is natural he should regard them as concrete and 'objective', since for his mentality there exists only this and nothing more -- in himself. In others he at once sees "imagination" at work. A too extraverted attitude may actually become so regardless of the subject that the latter is entirely sacrificed to so-called objective claims; to the demands, for instance, of a continually extending business, because orders lie claiming one's attention or because profitable possibilities are constantly being opened up which must instantly be seized.

This is the extravert's danger; he becomes caught up in objects, wholly losing himself in their toils. The functional (nervous) or actual physical disorders which result from this state have a compensatory significance, forcing the subject to an involuntary self-restriction. Should the symptoms be functional, their peculiar formation may symbolically express the psychological situation; a singer, for instance, whose fame quickly reaches a dangerous pitch tempting him to a disproportionate outlay of energy, is suddenly robbed of his high tones by a nervous inhibition. A man of very modest beginnings rapidly reaches a social position of great influence and wide prospects, when suddenly he is overtaken by a psychogenic state, with all the symptoms of mountain-sickness. Again, a man on the point of marrying an idolized woman of doubtful character, whose value he extravagantly over-estimates, is seized with a spasm of the oesophagus, which forces him to a regimen of two cups of milk in the day, demanding his threehourly attention. All visits to his fianceé are thus effectually stopped, and no choice is left to him but to busy himself with his bodily nourishment. A man who through his own energy and enterprise has built up a vast business, entailing an intolerable burden of work, is afflicted by nervous attacks of thirst, as a result of which he speedily falls a victim to hysterical alcoholism.

Hysteria is, in my view, by far the most frequent neurosis with the extraverted type. The classical example of hysteria is always characterized by an exaggerated rapport with the members of his circle, and a frankly imitatory accommodation to surrounding conditions. A constant tendency to appeal for interest and to produce impressions upon his milieu is a basic trait of the hysterical nature. A correlate to this is his proverbial suggestibility, his pliability to another person's influence. Unmistakable extraversion comes out in the communicativeness of the hysteric, which occasionally leads to the divulging of purely phantastic contents; whence arises the reproach of the hysterical lie.

To begin with, the 'hysterical' character is an exaggeration of the normal attitude; it is then complicated by compensatory reactions from the side of the unconscious, which manifests its opposition to the extravagant extraversion in the form of physical disorders, whereupon an introversion of psychic energy becomes unavoidable. Through this reaction of the unconscious, another category of symptoms arises which have a more introverted character. A morbid intensification of phantasy activity belongs primarily to this category. From this general characterization of the extraverted attitude, let us now turn to a description of the modifications, which the basic psychological functions undergo as a result of this attitude.

(II) THE ATTITUDE OF THE UNCONSCIOUS

It may perhaps seem odd that I should speak of attitude of the 'unconscious'. As I have already sufficiently indicated, I regard the relation of the unconscious to the conscious as compensatory. The unconscious, according to this view, has as good a claim to an I attitude' as the conscious.

In the foregoing section I emphasized the tendency to a certain one-sidedness in the extraverted attitude, due to the controlling power of the objective factor in the course, of psychic events. The extraverted type is constantly tempted to give himself away (apparently) in favour of the object, and to assimilate his subject to the object. I have referred in detail to the ultimate consequences of this exaggeration of the extraverted attitude, viz. to the injurious suppression of the subjective factor. It is only, to be expected, therefore, that a psychic compensation of the conscious extraverted attitude will lay especial weight upon the subjective factor, *i.e.* we shall have to prove a strong egocentric tendency in the unconscious. Practical experience actually furnishes this proof. I do not wish to enter into a casuistical survey at this point, so must refer my readers to the ensuing sections, where I shall attempt to present the characteristic attitude of the unconscious from the angle of each function-type, In this section we are merely concerned with the compensation of a general extraverted attitude; I shall, therefore, confine myself to an equally general characterization of the compensating attitude of the unconscious.

The attitude of the unconscious as an effective complement to the conscious extraverted attitude has a definitely introverting character. It focusses libido upon the subjective factor, *i.e.* all those needs and claims which are stifled or repressed by a too extraverted conscious attitude. It may be readily gathered from what has been said in the previous section that a purely objective orientation does violence to a multitude of subjective emotions, intentions, needs, and desires, since it robs them of the energy which is their natural right. Man is not a machine that one can reconstruct, as occasion demands, upon other lines and for quite other ends, in the hope that it will then proceed to function, in a totally different way, just as normally as before. Man bears his age-long history with him in his very structure is written the history of mankind.

The historical factor represents a vital need, to which a wise economy must respond. Somehow the past must become vocal, and participate in the present. Complete assimilation to the object, therefore, encounters the protest of the suppressed minority, elements belonging to the past and existing from the beginning. From this quite general consideration it may be understood why it is that the unconscious claims of the extraverted type have an essentially primitive, infantile, and egoistical character. When Freud says that the unconscious is "only able to wish", this observation contains a large measure of truth for the unconscious of the extraverted type. Adjustment and assimilation to objective data prevent inadequate subjective impulses from reaching consciousness. These tendencies (thoughts, wishes, affects, needs, feelings, etc.) take on a regressive character corresponding with the degree of their repression, ie. the less they are recognized, the more infantile and archaic they become. The conscious attitude robs them of their relatively disposable energycharge, only leaving them the energy of which it cannot deprive them. This remainder, which still possesses a potency not to be under-estimated, can be described only as primeval instinct. Instinct can never be rooted out from an individual by any arbitrary measures; it requires the slow, organic transformation of many generations to effect a radical change, for instinct is the energic [sic] expression of a definite organic foundation.

Thus with every repressed tendency a considerable sum of energy ultimately remains. This sum corresponds with the potency of the instinct and guards its effectiveness, notwithstanding the deprivation of energy which made it unconscious. The measure of extraversion in the conscious attitude entails a like degree of infantilism and archaism in the attitude of the unconscious. The egoism which so often characterizes the extravert's unconscious attitude goes far beyond mere childish selfishness; it even verges upon the wicked and brutal. It is here we find in fullest bloom that incest-wish described by Freud. It is self-evident that these things are entirely unconscious, remaining altogether hidden from the eyes of the uninitiated observer so long as the extraversion of the conscious attitude does not reach an extreme stage. But wherever an exaggeration of the conscious standpoint takes place, the unconscious also comes to light in a symptomatic form, *i.e.* the unconscious egoism, infantilism, and archaism lose their original compensatory characters, and appear in more or less open opposition to the conscious attitude. This process begins in the form of an absurd exaggeration of the conscious standpoint, which is aimed at a further repression of the unconscious, but usually ends in a reductio ad absurdum of the conscious attitude, *i.e.* a collapse. The catastrophe may be an objective one, since the objective aims gradually become falsified by the subjective. I remember the case of a printer who, starting as a mere employé, worked his way up through two decades of hard struggle, till at last he was the independent possessor of a very extensive business. The more the business extended, the more it increased its hold upon him, until gradually every other interest was allowed to become merged in it. At length he was completely enmeshed in its toils, and, as we shall soon see, this surrender eventually proved his ruin. As a sort of compensation to his exclusive interest in the business, certain memories of his childhood came to life. As a child he had taken great delight in painting and drawing. But, instead of renewing this capacity for its own sake as a balancing sideinterest, he canalized it into his business and began to conceive 'artistic' elaborations of his products. His phantasies unfortunately materialized: he actually began to produce after his own primitive and infantile taste, with the result that after a very few years his business went to pieces. He acted in obedience to one of our 'civilized ideals', which enjoins the energetic man to concentrate everything upon the one end in view. But he went too far, and merely fell a victim to the power of his subjective infantile claims.

But the catastrophic solution may also be subjective, *i.e.* in the form of a nervous collapse. Such a solution always comes about as a result of the unconscious counterinfluence, which can ultimately paralyse conscious action. In which case the claims of the unconscious force themselves categorically upon consciousness, thus creating a calamitous cleavage which generally reveals itself in two ways: either the subject no longer knows what he really wants and nothing any longer interests him, or he wants too much at once and has too keen an interest-but in impossible things. The suppression of infantile and primitive claims, which is often necessary on "civilized" grounds, easily leads to neurosis, or to the misuse of narcotics such as alcohol, morphine, cocaine, etc. In more extreme cases the cleavage ends in suicide.

It is a salient peculiarity of unconscious tendencies that, just in so far as they are deprived of their energy by *a lack of conscious recognition,* they assume a correspondingly destructive character, and as soon as this happen their compensatory function ceases. They cease to have a compensatory effect as soon as they reach a depth or stratum that corresponds with a level of culture absolutely incompatible with our own. From this moment the unconscious tendencies form a block, which is opposed to the conscious attitude in every respect ; such a bloc inevitably leads to open conflict.

In a general way, the compensating attitude of the unconscious finds expression in the process of psychic equilibrium. A normal extraverted attitude does not, of course, mean that the individual behaves invariably in accordance with the extraverted schema. Even in the same individual many psychological happenings may be observed, in which the mechanism of introversion is concerned. A habitus can be called extraverted only when the mechanism of extraversion predominates. In such a case the most highly differentiated function has a constantly extraverted application, while the inferior functions are found in the service of introversion, i.e. the more valued function, because the more conscious, is more completely subordinated to conscious control and purpose, whilst the less conscious, in other words, the partly unconscious inferior functions are subjected to conscious free choice in a much smaller degree.

The superior function is always the expression of the conscious personality, its aim, its will, and its achievement, whilst the inferior functions belong to the things that happen to one. Not that they merely beget blunders, *e.g.* lapsus linguae or lapsus calami, but they may also breed half or three-quarter resolves, since the inferior functions also possess a slight degree of consciousness. The extraverted feeling type is a classical example of this, for he enjoys an excellent feeling rapport with his entourage, yet occasionally opinions of an incomparable tactlessness will just happen to him. These opinions have their source in his inferior and subconscious thinking, which is only partly subject to control and is insufficiently related to the object ; to a large extent, therefore, it can operate without consideration or responsibility.

In the extraverted attitude the inferior functions always reveal a highly subjective determination with pronounced egocentricity and personal bias, thus demonstrating their close connection with the unconscious. Through their agency the unconscious is continually coming to light. On no account should we imagine that the unconscious lies permanently buried under so many overlying strata that it can only be uncovered, so to speak, by a laborious process of excavation. On the contrary, there is a constant influx of the unconscious into the conscious psychological process; at times this reaches such a pitch that the observer can decide only with difficulty which character-traits are to be ascribed to the conscious, and which to the unconscious personality. This difficulty occurs mainly with persons whose habit of expression errs rather on the side of profuseness. Naturally it depends very largely also upon the attitude of the observer, whether he lays hold of the conscious or the unconscious character of a personality. Speaking generally a judging observer will tend to seize the conscious character, while a perceptive observer will be influenced more by the unconscious character, since judgement is chiefly interested in the conscious motivation of the psychic process, while perception tends to register the mere happening. But in so far as we apply perception and judgment in equal measure, it may easily happen that a personality appears to us as both introverted and extraverted, so that we cannot at once decide to which attitude the superior function belongs. In such cases only a thorough analysis of the function qualities can help us to a sound opinion. During the analysis we must observe which function is placed under the control and motivation of consciousness, and which functions have an accidental and spontaneous character. The former is always more highly differentiated than the latter, which also possess many infantile and primitive qualities. Occasionally the former function gives the impression of normality, while the latter have something abnormal or pathological about them.

(III) THE PECULIARITIES OF THE BASIC PSYCHOLOGICAL FUNCTIONS IN THE EXTRAVERTED ATTITUDE

1. Thinking

As a result of the general attitude of extraversion, thinking is orientated by the object and objective data. This orientation of thinking produces a noticeable peculiarity.

Thinking in general is fed from two sources, firstly from subjective and in the last resort unconscious roots, and secondly from objective data transmitted through sense perceptions.

Extraverted thinking is conditioned in a larger measure by these latter factors than by the former. judgment always presupposes a criterion ; for the extraverted judgment, the valid and determining criterion is the standard taken from objective conditions, no matter whether this be directly represented by an objectively perceptible fact, or expressed in an objective idea ; for an objective idea, even when subjectively sanctioned, is equally external and objective in origin. Extraverted thinking, therefore, need not necessarily be a merely concretistic thinking it may equally well be a purely ideal thinking, if, for instance, it can be shown that the ideas with which it is engaged are to a great extent borrowed from without, i.e. are transmitted by tradition and education. The criterion of judgment, therefore, as to whether or no a thinking is extraverted, hangs directly upon the question: by [p. 429] which standard is its judgment governed -- is it furnished from without, or is its origin subjective? A further criterion is afforded by the direction of the thinker's conclusion, namely, whether or no the thinking has a preferential direction outwards. It is no proof of its extraverted nature that it is preoccupied with concrete objects, since I may be engaging my thoughts with a concrete object, either because I am abstracting my thought from it or because I am concretizing my thought with it. Even if I engage my thinking with concrete things, and to that extent could be described as extraverted, it yet remains both questionable and characteristic as regards the direction my thinking will take; namely, whether in its further course it leads back again to objective data, external facts, and generally accepted ideas, or not. So far as the practical thinking of the merchant, the engineer, or the natural science pioneer is concerned, the objective direction is at once manifest. But in the case of a philosopher it is open to doubt, whenever the course of his thinking is directed towards ideas. In such a case, before deciding, we must further enquire whether these ideas are mere abstractions from objective experience, in which case they would merely represent higher collective concepts, comprising a sum of objective facts ; or whether (if they are clearly not abstractions from immediate experience) they may not be derived from tradition or borrowed from the intellectual atmosphere of the time. In the latter event, such ideas must also belong to the category of objective data, in which case this thinking should also be called extraverted.

Although I do not propose to present the nature of introverted thinking at this point, reserving it for a later section, it is, however, essential that I should make a few statements about it before going further. For if one considers strictly what I have just said concerning [p. 430] extraverted thinking, one might easily conclude that such a statement includes everything that is generally understood as thinking. It might indeed be argued that a thinking whose aim is concerned neither with objective facts nor with general ideas scarcely merits the name 'thinking'. I am fully aware of the fact that the thought of our age, in common with its most eminent representatives, knows and acknowledges only the extraverted type of thinking. This is partly due to the fact that all thinking which attains visible form upon the world's surface, whether as science, philosophy, or even art, either proceeds direct from objects or flows into general ideas. On either ground, although not always completely evident it at least appears essentially intelligible, and therefore relatively valid. In this sense it might be said that the extraverted intellect, i.e. the mind that is orientated by objective data, is actually the only one recognized.

There is also, however -- and now I come to the question of the introverted intellect -- an entirely different kind of thinking, to which the term I "thinking" can hardly be denied: it is a kind that is neither orientated by the immediate objective experience nor is it concerned with general and objectively derived ideas. I reach this other kind of thinking in the following way. When my thoughts are engaged with a concrete object or general idea in such a way that the course of my thinking eventually leads me back again to my object, this intellectual process is not the only psychic proceeding taking place in me at the moment. I will disregard all those possible sensations and feelings which become noticeable as a more or less disturbing accompaniment to my train of thought, merely emphasizing the fact that this very thinking process which proceeds from objective data and strives again towards the object stands also in a constant relation to the subject. This relation is a condition sine qua non, without which no thinking process whatsoever could take place. Even though my thinking process is directed, as far as possible, towards objective data, nevertheless it is *my* subjective process, and it can neither escape the subjective admixture nor yet dispense with it. Although I try my utmost to give a completely objective direction to my train of thought, even then I cannot exclude the parallel subjective process with its all-embracing participation, without extinguishing the very spark of life from my thought. This parallel subjective process has a natural tendency, only relatively avoidable, to subjectify objective facts, *i.e.* to assimilate them to the subject.

Whenever the chief value is given to the subjective process, that other kind of thinking arises which stands opposed to extraverted thinking, namely, that purely subjective orientation of thought which I have termed introverted. A thinking arises from this other orientation that is neither determined by objective facts nor directed towards objective data -- a thinking, therefore, that proceeds from subjective data and is directed towards subjective ideas or facts of a subjective character. I do not wish to enter more fully into this kind of thinking here; I have merely established its existence for the purpose of giving a necessary complement to the extraverted thinking process, whose nature is thus brought to a clearer focus.

When the objective orientation receives a certain predominance, the thinking is extraverted. This circumstance changes nothing as regards the logic of thought -- it merely determines that difference between thinkers which James regards as a matter of temperament. The orientation towards the object, as already explained, makes no essential change in the thinking function; only its appearance is altered. Since it is governed by objective data, it has the appearance of being captivated by the object, as though without the external orientation it simply could not [p. 432] exist. Almost it seems as though it were a sequence of external facts, or as though it could reach its highest point only when chiming in with some generally valid idea. It seems constantly to be affected by objective data, drawing only those conclusions which substantially agree with these. Thus it gives one the impression of a certain lack of freedom, of occasional shortsightedness, in spite of every kind of adroitness within the objectively circumscribed area. What I am now describing is merely the impression this sort of thinking makes upon the observer, who must himself already have a different standpoint, or it would be quite impossible for him to observe the phenomenon of extraverted thinking. As a result of his different standpoint he merely sees its aspect, not its nature; whereas the man who himself possesses this type of thinking is able to seize its nature, while its aspect escapes him. judgment made upon appearance only cannot be fair to the essence of the thing-hence the result is depreciatory. But essentially this thinking is no less fruitful and creative than introverted thinking, only its powers are in the service of other ends. This difference is perceived most clearly when extraverted thinking is engaged upon material, which is specifically an object of the subjectively orientated thinking. This happens, for instance, when a subjective conviction is interpreted analytically from objective facts or is regarded as a product or derivative of objective ideas. But, for our 'scientifically' orientated consciousness, the difference between the two modes of thinking becomes still more obvious when the subjectively orientated thinking makes an attempt to bring objective data into connections not objectively given, *i.e.* to subordinate them to a subjective idea. Either senses the other as an encroachment, and hence a sort of shadow effect is produced, wherein either type reveals to the other its least favourable aspect, The subjectively orientated thinking then appears quite arbitrary, while the extraverted thinking seems to have an incommensurability that is altogether dull and banal. Thus the two standpoints are incessantly at war.

Such a conflict, we might think, could be easily adjusted if only we clearly discriminated objects of a subjective from those of an objective nature. Unfortunately, however, such a discrimination is a matter of impossibility, although not a few have attempted it. Even if such a separation were possible, it would be a very disastrous proceeding, since in themselves both orientations are onesided, with a definitely restricted validity; hence they both require this mutual correction. Thought is at once sterilized, whenever thinking is brought, to any great extent, under the influence of objective data, since it becomes degraded into a mere appendage of objective facts; in which case, it is no longer able to free itself from objective data for the purpose of establishing an abstract idea. The process of thought is reduced to mere 'reflection', not in the sense of 'meditation', but in the sense of a mere imitation that makes no essential affirmation beyond what was already visibly and immediately present in the objective data. Such a thinking-process leads naturally and directly back to the objective fact, but never beyond it ; not once, therefore, can it lead to the coupling of experience with an objective idea. And, vice versa, when this thinking has an objective idea for its object, it is quite unable to grasp the practical individual experience, but persists in a more or less tautological position. The materialistic mentality presents a magnificent example of this.

When, as the result of a reinforced objective determination, extraverted thinking is subordinated to objective data, it entirely loses itself, on the one hand, in the individual experience, and proceeds to amass an accumulation of undigested empirical material. The oppressive mass of more or less disconnected individual experiences produces a state of intellectual dissociation, which, on the other hand, usually demands a psychological compensation. This must consist in an idea, just as simple as it is universal, which shall give coherence to the heaped-up but intrinsically disconnected whole, or at least it should provide an inkling of such a connection. Such ideas as "matter" or "energy" are suitable for this purpose. But, whenever thinking primarily depends not so much upon external facts as upon an accepted or second-hand idea, the very poverty of the idea provokes a compensation in the form of a still more impressive accumulation of facts, which assume a one-sided grouping in keeping with the relatively restricted and sterile point of view; whereupon many valuable and sensible aspects of things automatically go by the board. The vertiginous abundance of the socalled scientific literature of to-day owes a deplorably high percentage of its existence to this misorientation.

2. The Extraverted Thinking Type

It is a fact of experience that all the basic psychological functions seldom or never have the same strength or grade of development in one and the same individual. As a rule, one or other function predominates, in both strength and development. When *supremacy* among the psychological functions is given to thinking, *i.e.* when the life of an individual is mainly ruled by reflective thinking so that every important action proceeds from intellectually considered motives, or when there is at least a tendency to conform to such motives, we may fairly call this a *thinking type*. Such a type can be either introverted or extraverted. We will first discuss the *extraverted thinking type*.

In accordance with his definition, we must picture a, man whose constant aim -- in so far, of course, as he is a pure type -- is to bring his total life-activities into relation with intellectual conclusions, which in the last resort are always orientated by objective data, whether objective facts or generally valid ideas. This type of man gives the deciding voice-not merely for himself alone but also on behalf of his entourage-either to the actual objective reality or to its objectively orientated, intellectual formula. By this formula are good and evil measured, and beauty and ugliness determined. All is right that corresponds with this formula; all is wrong that contradicts it; and everything that is neutral to it is purely accidental. Because this formula seems to correspond with the meaning of the world, it also becomes a world law whose realization must be achieved at all times and seasons, both individually and collectively. Just as the extraverted thinking type subordinates himself to his formula, so, for its own good, must his entourage also obey it, since the man who refuses to obey is wrong -- he is resisting the world-law, and is, therefore, unreasonable, immoral, and without a conscience. His moral code forbids him to tolerate exceptions; his ideal must, under all circumstances, be realized; for in his eyes it is the purest conceivable formulation of objective reality, and, therefore, must also be generally valid truth, quite indispensable for the salvation of man. This is not from any great love for his neighbour, but from a higher standpoint of justice and truth. Everything in his own nature that appears to invalidate this formula is mere imperfection, an accidental miss-fire, something to be eliminated on the next occasion, or, in the event of further failure, then clearly a sickness.

If tolerance for the sick, the suffering, or the deranged should chance to be an ingredient in the formula, special provisions will be devised for humane societies, hospitals, prisons, colonies, etc., or at least extensive plans for such projects. For the actual execution of these schemes the motives of justice and truth do not, as a rule, suffice; still devolve upon real Christian charity, which I to do with feeling than with any intellectual 'One really should' or I one must' figure largely in this programme. If the formula is wide enough, it may play a very useful rôle in social life, with a reformer or a ventilator of public wrongs or a purifier of the public conscience, or as the propagator of important innovations. But the more rigid the formula, the more, does he develop into a grumbler, a crafty reasoner, and a self-righteous critic, who would like to impress both himself and others into one schema.

We have now outlined two extreme figures, between which terminals the majority of these types may be graduated.

In accordance with the nature of the extraverted attitude, the influence and activities of such personalities are all the more favourable and beneficent, the further one goes from the centre. Their best aspect is to be found at the periphery of their sphere of influence. The further we penetrate into their own province, the more do the unfavourable results of their tyranny impress us. Another life still pulses at the periphery, where the truth of the formula can be sensed as an estimable adjunct to the rest. But the further we probe into the special sphere where the formula operates, the more do we find life ebbing away from all that fails to coincide with its dictates. Usually it is the nearest relatives who have to taste the most disagreeable results of an extraverted formula, since they are the first to be unmercifully blessed with it. But above all the subject himself is the one who suffers most -- which brings us to the other side of the psychology of this type.

The fact that an intellectual formula never has been and never will be discovered which could embrace the possibilities of life in a fitting expression must lead -- where such a formula is accepted -- to an inhibition, or total exclusion, of other highly important forms and activities of life. In the first place, all those vital forms dependent upon feeling will become repressed in such a type, as, for instance, aesthetic activities, taste, artistic sense, the art of friendship, etc. Irrational forms, such as religious experiences, passions and the like, are often obliterated even to the point of complete unconsciousness. These, conditionally quite important, forms of life have to support an existence that is largely unconscious. Doubtless there are exceptional men who are able to sacrifice their entire life to one definite formula; but for most of us a permanent life of such exclusiveness is impossible. Sooner or later -- in accordance with outer circumstances and inner gifts -- the forms of life repressed by the intellectual attitude become indirectly perceptible, through a gradual disturbance of the conscious conduct of life. Whenever disturbances of this kind reach a definite intensity, one speaks of a neurosis. In most cases, however, it does not go so far, because the individual instinctively allows himself some preventive extenuations of his formula, worded, of course, in a suitable and reasonable way. In this way a safety-valve is created.

The relative or total unconsciousness of such tendencies or functions as are excluded from any participation in the conscious attitude keeps them in a relatively undeveloped state. As compared with the conscious function they are inferior. To the extent that they are unconscious, they become merged with the remaining contents of the unconscious, from which they acquire a bizarre character. To the extent that they are conscious, they only play a secondary rôle, although one of considerable importance for the whole psychological picture.

Since feelings are the first to oppose and contradict the rigid intellectual formula, they are affected first this conscious inhibition, and upon them the most intense repression falls. No function can be entirely eliminated -- it can only be greatly distorted. In so far as feelings allow themselves to be arbitrarily shaped and subordinated, they have to support the intellectual conscious attitude and adapt themselves to its aims. Only to a certain degree, however, is this possible; a part of the feeling remains insubordinate, and therefore must be repressed. Should the repression succeed, it disappears from consciousness and proceeds to unfold a subconscious activity, which runs counter to conscious aims, even producing effects whose causation is a complete enigma to the individual. For example, conscious altruism, often of an extremely high order, may be crossed by a secret self-seeking, of which the individual is wholly unaware, and which impresses intrinsically unselfish actions with the stamp of selfishness. Purely ethical aims may lead the individual into critical situations, which sometimes have more than a semblance of being decided by quite other than ethical motives. There are guardians of public morals or voluntary rescue-workers who suddenly find themselves in deplorably compromising situations, or in dire need of rescue. Their resolve to save often leads them to employ means which only tend to precipitate what they most desire to avoid. There are extraverted idealists, whose desire to advance the salvation of man is so consuming that they will not shrink from any lying and dishonest means in the pursuit of their ideal. There are a few painful examples in science where investigators of the highest esteem, from a profound conviction of the truth and general validity of their formula, have not scrupled to falsify evidence in favour of their ideal. This is sanctioned by the formula; the end justifieth the means. Only an inferior feeling-function, operating seductively and unconsciously, could bring about such aberrations in otherwise reputable men.

The inferiority of feeling in this type manifests itself also in other ways. In so far as it corresponds with the dominating positive formula, the conscious attitude becomes more or less impersonal, often, indeed, to such a degree that a very considerable wrong is done to personal interests. When the conscious attitude is extreme, all personal considerations recede from view, even those which concern the individual's own person. His health is neglected, his social position deteriorates, often the most vital interests of his family are violated -- they are wronged morally and financially, even their bodily health is made to suffer -- all in the service of the ideal. At all events personal sympathy with others must be impaired, unless they too chance to be in the service of the same formula. Hence it not infrequently happens that his immediate family circle, his own children for instance, only know such a father as a cruel tyrant, whilst the outer world resounds with the fame of his humanity. Not so much in spite of as because of the highly impersonal character of the conscious attitude, the unconscious feelings are highly personal and oversensitive, giving rise to certain secret prejudices, as, for instance, a decided readiness to misconstrue any objective opposition to his formula as personal ill-will, or a constant tendency to make negative suppositions regarding the qualities of others in order to invalidate their arguments beforehand-in defence, naturally, of his own susceptibility. As a result of this unconscious sensitiveness, his expression and tone frequently becomes sharp, pointed, aggressive, and insinuations multiply. The feelings have an untimely and halting character, which is always a mark of the inferior function. Hence arises a pronounced tendency to resentment. However generous the individual sacrifice to the intellectual goal may be, the feelings are correspondingly petty, suspicious, crossgrained, and conservative. Everything new that is not already contained formula is viewed through a veil of unconscious and is judged accordingly. It happened only in middle of last century that a certain physician, famed his humanitarianism, threatened to dismiss an assistant for daring to use a thermometer, because the formula decreed that fever shall be recognized by the pulse. There are, of course, a host of similar examples.

Thinking which in other respects may be altogether blameless becomes all the more subtly and prejudicially, affected, the more feelings are repressed. An intellectual standpoint, which, perhaps on account of its actual intrinsic value, might justifiably claim general recognition, undergoes a characteristic alteration through the influence of this unconscious personal sensitiveness; it becomes rigidly dogmatic. The personal self-assertion is transferred to the intellectual standpoint. Truth is no longer left to work her natural effect, but through an identification with the subject she is treated like a sensitive darling whom an evil-minded critic has wronged. The critic is demolished, if possible with personal invective, and no argument is too gross to be used against him. Truth must be trotted out, until finally it begins to dawn upon the public that it is not so much really a question of truth as of her personal procreator.

The dogmatism of the intellectual standpoint, however, occasionally undergoes still further peculiar modifications from the unconscious admixture of unconscious personal feelings; these changes are less a question of feeling, in the stricter sense, than of contamination from other unconscious factors which become blended with the repressed feeling in the unconscious. Although reason itself offers proof, that every intellectual formula can be no more than a partial truth, and can never lay claim, therefore, to autocratic authority; in practice, the formula obtains so great an ascendancy that, beside it, every other standpoint and possibility recedes into the background. It replaces all the more general, less defined, hence the more modest and truthful, views of life. It even takes the place of that general view of life which we call religion. Thus the formula becomes a religion, although in essentials it has not the smallest connection with anything religious. Therewith it also gains the essentially religious character of absoluteness. It becomes, as it were, an intellectual superstition. But now all those psychological tendencies that suffer under its repression become grouped together in the unconscious, and form a counter-position, giving rise to paroxysms of doubt. As a defence against doubt, the conscious attitude grows fanatical. For fanaticism, after all, is merely overcompensated doubt. Ultimately this development leads to an exaggerated defence of the conscious position, and to the gradual formation of an absolutely antithetic unconscious position; for example, an extreme irrationality develops, in opposition to the conscious rationalism, or it becomes highly archaic and superstitious, in opposition to a conscious standpoint imbued with modern science. This fatal opposition is the source of those narrow-minded and ridiculous views, familiar to the historians of science, into which many praiseworthy pioneers have ultimately blundered. It not infrequently happens in a man of this type that the side of the unconscious becomes embodied in a woman.

In my experience, this type, which is doubtless familiar to my readers, is chiefly found among men, since thinking tends to be a much more dominant function in men than in women. As a rule, when thinking achieves the mastery in women, it is, in my experience, a kind of thinking which results from a prevailingly *intuitive* activity of mind.

The thought of the extraverted thinking type is, *positive,* i.e. it produces. It either leads to new facts or to general conceptions of disparate experimental material. Its judgment is generally *synthetic.* Even when it analyses, it constructs, because it is always advancing beyond the, analysis to a new combination, a further conception which reunites the analysed material in a new way or adds some., thing further to the given material. In general, therefore, we may describe this kind of judgment as predicative. In any case, characteristic that it is never absolutely depreciatory or destructive, but always substitutes a fresh value for one that is demolished. This quality is due to the fact that thought is the main channel into which a thinkingtype's energy flows. Life steadily advancing shows itself in the man's thinking, so that his ideas maintain a progressive, creative character. His thinking neither stagnates, nor is it in the least regressive. Such qualities cling only to a thinking that is not given priority in consciousness. In this event it is relatively unimportant, and also lacks the character of a positive vital activity. It follows in the wake of other functions, it becomes Epimethean, it has an 'esprit de l'escalier' quality, contenting itself with constant ponderings and broodings upon things past and gone, in an effort to analyse and digest them. Where the creative element, as in this case, inhabits another function, thinking no longer progresses it stagnates. Its judgment takes on a decided *inherencycharacter,* i.e. it entirely confines itself to the range of the given material, nowhere overstepping it. It is contented with a more or less abstract statement, and fails to impart any value to the experimental material that was not already there.

The inherency-judgment of such extraverted thinking is objectively orientated, *i.e.* its conclusion always expresses the objective importance of experience. Hence, not only does it remain under the orientating influence of objective data, but it actually rests within the charmed circle of the individual experience, about which it affirms nothing that was not already given by it. We may easily observe this thinking in those people who cannot refrain from tacking on to an impression or experience some rational and doubtless very valid remark, which, however, in no way adventures beyond the given orbit of the experience. At bottom, such a remark merely says 'I have understood it -- I can reconstruct it.' But there the matter also ends. At its very highest, such a judgment signifies merely the placing of an experience in an objective setting, whereby the experience is at once recognized as belonging to the frame.

But whenever a function other than thinking possesses priority in consciousness to any marked degree, in so far as thinking is conscious at all and not directly dependent upon the dominant function, it assumes a *negative* character. In so far as it is subordinated to the dominant function, it may actually wear a positive aspect, but a narrower scrutiny will easily prove that it simply mimics the dominant function, supporting it with arguments that unmistakably contradict the laws of logic proper to thinking. Such a thinking, therefore, ceases to have any interest for our present discussion. Our concern is rather with the constitution of that thinking which cannot be subordinated to the dominance of another function, but remains true to its own principle. To observe and investigate this thinking in itself is not easy, since, in the concrete case, it is more or less constantly repressed by the conscious attitude. Hence, in the majority of cases, it first must be retrieved from the background of consciousness, unless in some unguarded moment it should chance to come accidentally to the surface. As a rule, it must be enticed with some such questions as 'Now what do you *really* think?' or, again, 'What is your private view about the matter?' Or perhaps one may even use a little cunning, framing the question something this: 'What do you imagine, then, that *I* really think about the matter?' This latter form should be chosen when the real thinking is unconscious and, therefore projected. The thinking that is enticed to the surface this way has characteristic qualities; it was these I had in mind just now when I described it as *negative.* It habitual mode is best characterized by the two words 'nothing but'. Goethe personified this thinking in the figure of Mephistopheles. It shows a most distinctive tendency to trace back the object of its judgment to some banality or other, thus stripping it of its own independent significance. This happens simply because it is represented as being dependent upon some other commonplace thing. Wherever a conflict, apparently essential in nature, arises between two men, negative thinking mutters 'Cherchez la femme'. When a man champions or advocates a cause, negative thinking makes no inquiry as to the importance of the thing, but merely asks 'How much does he make by it?' The dictum ascribed to Moleschott: "Der Mensch ist, was er isst" (" Man is what he eats ") also belongs to this collection, as do many more aphorisms and opinions which I need not enumerate.

The destructive quality of this thinking as well as its occasional and limited usefulness, hardly need further elucidation. But there still exists another form of negative thinking, which at first glance perhaps would scarcely be recognized as such I refer to the *theosophical* thinking which is to-day rapidly spreading in every quarter of the globe, presumably as a reaction phenomenon to the materialism of the epoch now receding. Theosophical thinking has an air that is not in the least reductive, since it exalts everything to transcendental and world-embracing ideas. A dream, for instance, is no [p. 445] longer a modest dream, but an experience upon 'another plane'. The hitherto inexplicable fact of telepathy is ,very simply explained by 'vibrations' which pass from one man to another. An ordinary nervous trouble is quite simply accounted for by the fact that something has collided with the astral body. Certain anthropological peculiarities of the dwellers on the Atlantic seaboard are easily explained by the submerging of Atlantis, and so on. We have merely to open a theosophical book to be overwhelmed by the realization that everything is already explained, and that 'spiritual science' has left no enigmas of life unsolved. But, fundamentally, this sort of thinking is just as negative as materialistic thinking. When the latter conceives psychology as chemical changes taking place in the cell-ganglia, or as the extrusion and withdrawal of cell-processes, or as an internal secretion, in essence this is just as superstitious as theosophy. The only difference lies in the fact that materialism reduces all phenomena to our current physiological notions, while theosophy brings everything into the concepts of Indian metaphysics. When we trace the dream to an overloaded stomach, the dream is not thereby explained, and when we explain telepathy as 'vibrations', we have said just as little. Since, what are 'vibrations'? Not only are both methods of explanation quite impotent -- they are actually destructive, because by interposing their seeming explanations they withdraw interest from the problem, diverting it in the former case to the stomach, and in the latter to imaginary vibrations, thus preventing any serious investigation of the problem. Either kind of thinking is both sterile and sterilizing. Their negative quality consists in this it is a method of thought that is indescribably cheap there is a real poverty of productive and creative energy. It is a thinking taken in tow by other functions.

3. Feeling

Feeling in the extraverted attitude is orientated by objective data, *i.e.* the object is the indispensable determinant of the kind of feeling. It agrees with objective values. If one has always known feeling as a subjective fact, the nature of extraverted feeling will not immediately be understood, since it has freed itself as fully as possible from the subjective factor, and has, instead, become wholly subordinated to the influence of the object. Even where it seems to show a certain independence of the quality of the concrete object, it is none the less under the spell of. traditional or generally valid standards of some sort. I may feel constrained, for instance, to use the predicate 'beautiful' or 'good', not because I find the object 'beautiful' or 'good' from my own subjective feeling, but because it is *fitting* and politic so to do; and fitting it certainly is, inasmuch as a contrary opinion would disturb the general feeling situation. A feeling-judgment such as this is in no way a simulation or a lie -- it is merely an act of accommodation. A picture, for instance, may be termed beautiful, because a picture that is hung in a drawing-room and bearing a well-known signature is generally assumed to be beautiful, or because the predicate 'ugly' might offend the family of the fortunate possessor, or because there is a benevolent intention on the part of the visitor to create a pleasant feeling-atmosphere, to which end everything must be felt as agreeable. Such feelings are governed by the standard of the objective determinants. As such they are genuine, and represent the total visible feeling-function.

In precisely the same way as extraverted thinking strives to rid itself of subjective influences, extraverted feeling has also to undergo a certain process of differentiation, before it is finally denuded of every subjective [p. 447] trimming. The *valuations* resulting from the act of feeling either correspond directly with objective values or at least chime in with certain traditional and generally known standards of value. This kind of feeling is very largely responsible for the fact that so many people flock to the theatre, to concerts, or to Church, and what is more, with correctly adjusted positive feelings. Fashions, too, owe their existence to it, and, what is far more valuable, the whole positive and wide-spread support of social, philanthropic, and such like cultural enterprises. In such matters, extraverted feeling proves itself a creative factor. Without this feeling, for instance, a beautiful and harmonious sociability would be unthinkable. So far extraverted feeling is just as beneficent and rationally effective as extraverted thinking. But this salutary effect is lost as soon as the object gains an exaggerated influence. For, when this happens, extraverted feeling draws the personality too much into the object, *i.e.* the object assimilates the person, whereupon the personal character of the feeling, which constitutes its principal charm, is lost. Feeling then becomes cold, material, untrustworthy. It betrays a secret aim, or at least arouses the suspicion of it in an impartial observer. No longer does it make that welcome and refreshing impression the invariable accompaniment of genuine feeling; instead, one scents a pose or affectation, although the egocentric motive may be entirely unconscious.

Such overstressed, extraverted feeling certainly fulfils æsthetic expectations, but no longer does it speak to the heart; it merely appeals to the senses, or -- worse still -- to the reason. Doubtless it can provide æsthetic padding for a situation, but there it stops, and beyond that its effect is nil. It has become sterile. Should this process go further, a strangely contradictory dissociation of feeling develops; every object is seized upon with feeling- valuations, and numerous relationships are made which are inherently and mutually incompatible. Since such aberrations would be quite impossible if a sufficiently emphasized subject were present, the last vestige of a real personal standpoint also becomes suppressed. The subject becomes so swallowed up in individual feeling processes that to the observer it seems as though there were no longer a subject of feeling but merely a feeling process. In such a condition feeling has entirely forfeited its original human warmth, it gives an impression of pose, inconstancy, unreliability, and in the worst cases appears definitely hysterical.

4. The Extraverted Feeling-Type

In so far as feeling is, incontestably, a more obvious peculiarity of feminine psychology than thinking, the most pronounced feeling-types are also to be found among women. When extraverted feeling possesses the priority we speak of an extraverted feeling-type. Examples of this type that I can call to mind are, almost without exception, women. She is a woman who follows the guiding-line of her feeling. As the result of education her feeling has become developed into an adjusted function, subject to conscious control. Except in extreme cases, feeling has a personal character, in spite of the fact that the subjective factor may be already, to a large extent, repressed. The personality appears to be adjusted in relation to objective conditions. Her feelings correspond with objective situations and general values. Nowhere is this more clearly revealed than in the so-called 'love-choice'; the 'suitable' man is loved, not another one; he is suitable not so much because he fully accords with the fundamental character of the woman -- as a rule she is quite uninformed about this -- but because [p. 449] he meticulously corresponds in standing, age, capacity, height, and family respectability with every reasonable requirement. Such a formulation might, of course, be easily rejected as ironical or depreciatory, were I not fully convinced that the love-feeling of this type of woman completely corresponds with her choice. It is genuine, and not merely intelligently manufactured. Such 'reasonable' marriages exist without number, and they are by no means the worst. Such women are good comrades to their husbands and excellent mothers, so long as husbands or children possess the conventional psychic constitution. One can feel 'correctly', however, only when feeling is disturbed by nothing else. But nothing disturbs feeling so much as thinking. It is at once intelligible, therefore, that this type should repress thinking as much as possible. This does not mean to say that such a woman does not think at all; on the contrary, she may even think a great deal and very ably, but her thinking is never sui generis; it is, in fact, an Epimethean appendage to her feeling. What she cannot feel, she cannot consciously think. 'But I can't think what I don't feel', such a type said to me once in indignant tones. As far as feeling permits, she can think very well, but every conclusion, however logical, that might lead to a disturbance of feeling is rejected from the outset. It is simply not thought. And thus everything that corresponds with objective valuations is good: these things are loved or treasured; the rest seems merely to exist in a world apart.

But a change comes over the picture when the importance of the object reaches a still higher level. As already explained above, such an assimilation of subject to object then occurs as almost completely to engulf the subject of feeling. Feeling loses its personal character -- it becomes feeling per se; it almost seems as though the [p. 450] personality were wholly dissolved in the feeling of the moment. Now, since in actual life situations constantly and successively alternate, in which the feeling-tones released are not only different but are actually mutually contrasting, the personality inevitably becomes dissipated in just so many different feelings. Apparently, he is this one moment, and something completely different the next -- apparently, I repeat, for in reality such a manifold personality is altogether impossible. The basis of the ego always remains identical with itself, and, therefore, appears definitely opposed to the changing states of feeling. Accordingly the observer senses the display of feeling not so much as a personal expression of the feeling-subject as an alteration of his ego, a mood, in other words. Corresponding with the degree of dissociation between the ego and the momentary state of feeling, signs of disunion with the self will become more or less evident, *i.e.* the original compensatory attitude of the unconscious becomes a manifest opposition. This reveals itself, in the first instance, in extravagant demonstrations of feeling, in loud and obtrusive feeling predicates, which leave one, however, somewhat incredulous. They ring hollow; they are not convincing. On the contrary, they at once give one an inkling of a resistance that is being overcompensated, and one begins to wonder whether such a feeling-judgment might not just as well be entirely different. In fact, in a very short time it actually *is* different. Only a very slight alteration in the situation is needed to provoke forthwith an entirely contrary estimation of the selfsame object. The result of such an experience is that the observer is unable to take either judgment at all seriously. He begins to reserve his own opinion. But since, with this type, it is a matter of the greatest moment to establish an intensive feeling rapport with his environment, redoubled efforts are now required to overcome this reserve. Thus, in the manner of the circulus vitiosus, the situation goes from bad to worse. The more the feeling relation with the object becomes overstressed, the nearer the unconscious opposition approaches the surface.

We have already seen that the extraverted feeling type, as a rule, represses his thinking, just because thinking is the function most liable to disturb feeling. Similarly, when thinking seeks to arrive at pure results of any kind, its first act is to exclude feeling, since nothing is calculated to harass and falsify thinking so much as feeling-values. Thinking, therefore, in so far as it is an independent function, is repressed in the extraverted feeling type. Its repression, as I observed before, is complete only in so far as its inexorable logic forces it to conclusions that are incompatible with feeling. It is suffered to exist as the servant of feeling, or more accurately its slave. Its backbone is broken; it may not operate on its own account, in accordance with its own laws, Now, since a logic exists producing inexorably right conclusions, this must happen somewhere, although beyond the bounds of consciousness, *i.e.* in the unconscious. Preeminently, therefore, the unconscious content of this type is a particular kind of thinking. It is an infantile, archaic, and negative thinking.

So long as conscious feeling preserves the personal character, or, in other words, so long as the personality does not become swallowed up by successive states of feeling, this unconscious thinking remains compensatory. But as soon as the personality is dissociated, becoming dispersed in mutually contradictory states of feeling, the identity of the ego is lost, and the subject becomes unconscious. But, because of the subject's lapse into the unconscious, it becomes associated with the unconscious thinking -- function, therewith assisting the unconscious thought to occasional consciousness. The stronger the conscious feeling relation, and therefore, the more 'depersonalized,' it becomes, the stronger grows the unconscious opposition. This reveals itself in the fact that unconscious ideas centre round just the most valued objects, which are thus pitilessly stripped of their value. That thinking which always thinks in the 'nothing but' style is in its right place here, since it destroys the ascendancy of the feeling that is chained to the object.

Unconscious thought reaches the surface in the form of irruptions, often of an obsessing nature, the general character of which is always negative and depreciatory. Women of this type have moments when the most hideous thoughts fasten upon the very objects most valued by their feelings. This negative thinking avails itself of every infantile prejudice or parallel that is calculated to breed doubt in the feeling-value, and it tows every primitive instinct along with it, in the effort to make 'a nothing but' interpretation of the feeling. At this point, it is perhaps in the nature of a side-remark to observe that the collective unconscious, *i.e.* the totality of the primordial images, also becomes enlisted in the same manner, and from the elaboration and development of these images there dawns the possibility of a regeneration of the attitude upon another basis.

Hysteria, with the characteristic infantile sexuality of its unconscious world of ideas, is the principal form of neurosis with this type.

5. Recapitulation of Extraverted Rational Types

I term the two preceding types rational or judging types because they are characterized by the supremacy of the reasoning and the judging functions. It is a general distinguishing mark of both types that their life is, to a large extent, subordinated to reasoning judgment. But we must not overlook the point, whether by 'reasoning' we are referring to the standpoint of the individual's subjective psychology, or to the standpoint of the observer, who perceives and judges from without. For such an observer could easily arrive at an opposite judgment, especially if he has a merely intuitive apprehension of the behaviour of the observed, and judges accordingly. In its totality, the life of this type is never dependent upon reasoning judgment alone; it is influenced in almost equal degree by unconscious irrationality. If observation is restricted to behaviour, without any concern for the domestic interior of the individual's consciousness, one may get an even stronger impression of the irrational and accidental character of certain unconscious manifestations in the individual's behaviour than of the reasonableness of his conscious purposes and motivations. I, therefore, base my judgment upon what the individual feels to be his conscious psychology. But I am prepared to grant that we may equally well entertain a precisely opposite conception of such a psychology, and present it accordingly. I am also convinced that, had I myself chanced to possess a different individual psychology, I should have described the rational types in the reversed way, from the standpoint of the unconscious-as irrational, therefore. This circumstance aggravates the difficulty of a lucid presentation of psychological matters to a degree not to be underestimated, and immeasurably increases the possibility of misunderstandings. The discussions which develop from these misunderstandings are, as a rule, quite hopeless, since the real issue is never joined, each side speaking, as it were, in a different tongue. Such experience is merely one reason the more for basing my presentation upon the subjective conscious psychology of the individual, since there, at least, one has a definite objective footing, which completely drops away the moment we try to ground psychological principles upon the unconscious. For the observed, in this case, could undertake no kind of co-operation, because there is nothing of which he is not more informed than his own unconscious. The judgment would entirely devolve upon the observer -- a certain guarantee that its basis would be his own individual psychology, which would infallibly be imposed upon the observed. To my mind, this is the case in the psychologies both of Freud and of Adler. The individual is completely

at the mercy of the arbitrary discretion of his observing critic -- which can never be the case when the conscious psychology of the observed is accepted as the basis.
After all, he is the only competent judge, since he alone knows his own motives.

The reasonableness that characterizes the conscious management of life in both these types, involves a conscious exclusion of the accidental and non-rational. Reasoning judgment, in such a psychology, represents a power that coerces the untidy and accidental things of life into definite forms; such at least is its aim. Thus, on the one hand, a definite choice is made among the possibilities of life, since only the rational choice is consciously accepted; but, on the other hand, the independence and influence of those psychic functions which perceive life's happenings are essentially restricted. This limitation of sensation and intuition is, of course, not absolute. These functions exist, for they are universal; but their products are subject to the choice of the reasoning judgment. It is not the absolute strength of sensation, for instance, which turns the scales in the motivation of action, but judgment, Thus, in a certain sense, the perceivingfunctions share the same fate as feeling in the case of the first type, or thinking in that of the second. They are relatively repressed, and therefore in an inferior state of differentiation. This circumstance gives a particular stamp to the unconscious of both our types; what such men do consciously and intentionally accords with reason (*their* reason of course), but what happens to them corresponds either with infantile, primitive sensations, or with similarly archaic intuitions. I will try to make clear what I mean by these latter concepts in the sections that follow. At all events, that which happens to this type is irrational (from their own standpoint of course). Now, since there are vast numbers of men whose lives consist in what happens to them more than in actions resulting from reasoned intention, it might conceivably happen, that such a man, after careful analysis, would describe both our types as irrational. We must grant him, however, that only too often a man's unconscious makes a far stronger impression upon one than his conscious, and that his actions often have considerably more weight and meaning than his reasoned motivations.

The rationality of both types is orientated objectively, and depends upon objective data. Their reasonableness corresponds with what passes as reasonable from the collective standpoint. Subjectively they consider nothing rational save what is generally considered as such. But reason is also very largely subjective and individual. In our case this share is repressed -- increasingly so, in fact, the more the significance of the object is exalted, Both the subject and subjective reason, therefore, are always threatened with repression and, when it descends, they fall under the tyranny of the unconscious, which in this case possesses most unpleasant qualities. We have already spoken of its thinking. But, in addition, there are primitive sensations, which reveal themselves in compulsive forms, as, for instance, an abnormal compulsive pleasure seeking in every conceivable direction ; there are also primitive intuitions, which can become a positive torture to the individuals concerned, not to mention their entourage. Everything disagreeable and painful, everything disgusting, ugly, and evil is scented out or suspected, and these as a rule only correspond with half-truths, than which nothing is more calculated to create misunderstandings of the most poisonous kind. The powerful influence of the opposing unconscious contents necessarily brings about a frequent interruption of the rational conscious government, namely, a striking subservience to the element of chance, so that, either by virtue of their sensational value or unconscious significance, accidental happenings acquire a compelling influence.

6. Sensation

Sensation, in the extraverted attitude, is most definitely conditioned by the object. As senseperception, sensation is naturally dependent upon the object. But, just as naturally, it is also dependent upon the subject; hence, there is also a subjective sensation, which after its kind is entirely different from the objective. In the extraverted attitude this subjective share of sensation, in so far as its conscious application is concerned, is either inhibited or repressed. As an irrational function, sensation is equally repressed, whenever a rational function, thinking or feeling, possesses the priority, ie. it can be said to have a conscious function, only in so far as the rational attitude of consciousness permits accidental perceptions to become conscious contents; in short, realizes them. The function of sense is, of course, absolute in the stricter sense; for example, everything is seen or heard to the farthest physiological possibility, but not everything attains that threshold value which a perception must possess in order to be also apperceived. It is a different matter when sensation itself possesses priority, instead of merely seconding another function. In this case, no element of objective sensation is excluded and nothing repressed (with the exception of the subjective share [p. 457] already mentioned). Sensation has a preferential objective determination, and those objects which release the strongest sensation are decisive for the individual's psychology. The result of this is a pronounced *sensuous hold* to the object. Sensation, therefore, is a vital function, equipped with the potentest [sic] vital instinct. In so far as objects release sensations, they matter; and, in so far as it lies within the power of sensation, they are also fully accepted into consciousness, whether compatible with reasoned judgment or not. As a function its sole criterion of value is the strength of the sensation as conditioned by its objective qualities. Accordingly, all objective processes, in so far as they release sensations at all, make their appearance in consciousness. It is, however, only concrete, sensuously perceived objects or processes which excite sensations in the extraverted attitude; exclusively those, in fact, which everyone in all times and places would sense as concrete. Hence, the orientation of such an individual corresponds with purely concrete reality. The judging, rational functions are subordinated to the concrete facts of sensation, and, accordingly, possess the qualities of inferior differentiation, *i.e.* they are marked by a certain negativity, with infantile and archaic tendencies. The function most affected by the repression, is, naturally, the one standing opposite to sensation, viz. intuition, the function of unconscious perception.

7. The Extraverted Sensation Type

No other human type can equal the extraverted sensation-type in realism. His sense for objective facts is extraordinarily developed. His life is an accumulation of actual experience with concrete objects, and the more pronounced he is, the less use does he make of his experience. In certain cases the events of his life hardly deserve [p. 458] the name 'experience'. He knows no better use for this sensed 'experience' than to make it serve as a guide to fresh sensations; anything in the least 'new' that comes within his circle of interest is forthwith turned to a sensational account and is made to serve this end. In so far as one is disposed to regard a highly developed sense for sheer actuality as very reasonable, will such men be esteemed rational. In reality, however, this is by no means the case, since they are equally subject to the sensation of irrational, chance happenings, as they are to rational behaviour.

Such a type -- the majority arc men apparently -- does not, of course, believe himself to be 'subject' to sensation. He would be much more inclined to ridicule this view as altogether inconclusive, since, from his standpoint, sensation is the concrete manifestation of life -- it is simply the fulness [sic] of actual living. His aim is concrete enjoyment, and his morality is similarly orientated. For true enjoyment has its own special morality, its own moderation and lawfulness, its own unselfishness and devotedness. It by no means follows that he is just sensual or gross, for he may differentiate his sensation to the finest pitch of æsthetic purity without being the least unfaithful, even in his most abstract sensations, to his principle of objective sensation.

Wulfen's *Cicerone des r¨cksichtlosen Lebensgenusses* is the unvarnished confession of a type of this sort. From this point of view the book seems to me worth reading.

Upon the lower levels this is the man of tangible reality, with little tendency either for reflection or commanding purpose. To sense the object, to have and if possible to enjoy sensations, is his constant motive. He is by no means unlovable; on the contrary, he frequently has a charming and lively capacity for enjoyment; he is sometimes a jolly fellow, and often a refined æsthete.

In the former case, the great problems of life hinge upon a good or indifferent dinner; in the latter, they are questions of good taste. When he 'senses', everything essential has been said and done. Nothing can be more than concrete and actual; conjectures that transcend or go beyond the concrete are only permitted on condition that they enhance sensation. This need not be in any way a pleasurable reinforcement, since this type is not a common voluptuary; he merely desires the strongest sensation, and this, by his very nature, he can receive only from without. What comes from within seems to him morbid and objectionable. In so far as lie thinks and feels, he always reduces down to objective foundations, *i.e.* to influences coming from the object, quite unperturbed by the most violent departures from logic. Tangible reality, under any conditions, makes him breathe again. In this respect he is unexpectedly credulous. He will, without hesitation, relate an obvious psychogenic symptom to the falling barometer, while the existence of a psychic conflict seems to him a fantastic abnormality. His love is incontestably rooted in the manifest attractions of the object. In so far as he is normal, he is conspicuously adjusted to positive reality -- conspicuously, because his adjustment is always visible. His ideal is the actual; in this respect he is considerate. He has no ideals related to ideas -- he has, therefore, no sort of ground for maintaining a hostile attitude towards the reality of things and facts. This expresses itself in all the externals of his life. He dresses well, according to his circumstances ; he keeps a good table for his friends, who are either made comfortable or at least given to understand that his fastidious taste is obliged to impose certain claims upon his entourage. He even convinces one that certain sacrifices are decidedly worth while for the sake of style.

But the more sensation predominates, so that the sensing subject disappears behind the sensation, the more unsatisfactory does this type become. Either he develops into a crude pleasure-seeker or he becomes an unscrupulous, designing sybarite. Although the object is entirely indispensable to him, yet, as something existing in and through itself, it is none the less depreciated. It is ruthlessly violated and essentially ignored, since now its sole use is to stimulate sensation. The hold upon the object is pushed to the utmost limit. The unconscious is, accordingly, forced out of its me[accent]tier as a compensatory function and driven into open opposition. But, above all, the repressed intuitions begin to assert themselves in the form of projections upon the object. The strangest conjectures arise; in the case of a sexual object, jealous phantasies and anxiety-states play a great role.

More acute cases develop every sort of phobia, and especially compulsive symptoms. The pathological contents have a remarkable air of unreality, with a frequent moral or religious colouring. A pettifogging captiousness often develops, or an absurdly scrupulous morality coupled with a primitive, superstitious and 'magical' religiosity, harking back to abstruse rites. All these things have their source in the repressed inferior functions, which, in such cases, stand in harsh opposition to the conscious standpoint; they wear, in fact, an aspect that is all the more striking because they appear to rest upon the most absurd suppositions, in complete contrast to the conscious sense of reality. The whole culture of thought and feeling seems, in this second personality, to be twisted into a morbid primitiveness; reason is hair-splitting sophistry -- morality is dreary moralizing and palpable Pharisaism -- religion is absurd superstition -- intuition, the noblest of human gifts, is a mere personal subtlety, a sniffing into every corner; instead of searching the horizon, it recedes to the narrowest gauge of human meanness.

The specially compulsive character of the neurotic symptoms represent the unconscious counterweight to the laisser aller morality of a purely sensational attitude, which, from the standpoint of rational judgment, accepts without discrimination, everything that happens. Although this lack of basic principles in the sensation-type does not argue an absolute lawlessness and lack of restraint, it at least deprives him of the quite essential restraining power of judgment. Rational judgment represents a conscious coercion, which the rational type appears to impose upon himself of his own free will. This compulsion overtakes the sensation-type from the unconscious. Moreover, the rational type's link to the object, from the very existence of a judgment, never means such an unconditioned relation as that which the sensation-type has with the object. When his attitude reaches an abnormal one-sidedness, he is in danger of falling just as deeply into the arms of the unconscious as he consciously clings to the object. When he becomes neurotic, he is much harder to treat in the rational way, because the functions to which the physician must appeal are in a relatively undifferentiated state; hence little or no trust can be placed in them. Special means of bringing emotional pressure to bear are often needed to make him at all conscious.

8. Intuition

Intuition as the function of unconscious perception is wholly directed upon outer objects in the extraverted attitude. Because, in the main, intuition is an unconscious process, the conscious apprehension of its nature is a very difficult matter. In consciousness, the intuitive function is represented by a certain attitude of expectation, a perceptive and penetrating vision, wherein only the subsequent result can prove, in every case, how much was [p. 462] 'perceived-into', and how much actually lay in the object.

Just as sensation, when given the priority, is not a mere reactive process of no further importance for the object, but is almost an action which seizes and shapes the object, so it is with intuition, which is by no means a mere perception, or awareness, but an active, creative process that builds into the object just as much as it takes out. But, because this process extracts the perception unconsciously, it also produces an unconscious effect in the object. The primary function of intuition is to transmit mere images, or perceptions of relations and conditions, which could be gained by the other functions, either not at all, or only by very roundabout ways. Such images have the value of definite discernments, and have a decisive bearing upon action, whenever intuition is given the chief weight; in which case, psychic adaptation is based almost exclusively upon intuition. Thinking, feeling, and sensation are relatively repressed; of these, sensation is the one principally affected, because, as the conscious function of sense, it offers the greatest obstacle to intuition. Sensation disturbs intuition's clear, unbiassed, na[umlaut]ive awareness with its importunate sensuous stimuli; for these direct the glance upon the physical superficies, hence upon the very things round and beyond which intuition tries to peer. But since intuition, in the extraverted attitude, has a prevailingly objective orientation, it actually comes very near to sensation; indeed, the expectant attitude towards outer objects may, with almost equal probability, avail itself of sensation. Hence, for intuition really to become paramount, sensation must to a large extent be suppressed. I am now speaking of sensation as the simple and direct sense-reaction, an almost definite physiological and psychic datum. This must be expressly established beforehand, because, if I ask the intuitive how he is [p. 463] orientated, he will speak of things which are quite indistinguishable from sense-perceptions. Frequently he will even make use of the term 'sensation'. He actually has sensations, but he is not guided by them per se, merely using them as directing-points for his distant vision. They are selected by unconscious expectation. Not the strongest sensation, in the physiological sense, obtains the crucial value, but any sensation whatsoever whose value happens to become considerably enhanced by reason of the intuitive's unconscious attitude. In this way it may eventually attain the leading position, appearing to the intuitive's consciousness indistinguishable from a pure sensation. But actually it is not so.

Just as extraverted sensation strives to reach the highest pitch of actuality, because only thus can the appearance of a complete life be created, so intuition tries to encompass the greatest *possibilities,* since only through the awareness of possibilities is *intuition* fullysatisfied. Intuition seeks to discover possibilities in the objective situation; hence as a mere tributary function (viz. when not in the position of priority) it is also the instrument which, in the presence of a hopelessly blocked situation, works automatically towards the issue, which no other function could discover. Where intuition has the priority, every ordinary situation in life seems like a closed room, which intuition has to open. It is constantly seeking outlets and fresh possibilities in external life. In a very short time every actual situation becomes a prison to the intuitive; it burdens him like a chain, prompting a compelling need for solution. At times objects would seem to have an almost exaggerated value, should they chance to represent the idea of a severance or release that might lead to the discovery of a new possibility. Yet no sooner have they performed their office, serving intuition as a ladder or a bridge, than they appear to have no further value, and are discarded as mere burdensome appendages. A fact is acknowledged only in so far as it opens up fresh possibilities of advancing beyond it and of releasing the individual from its operation. Emerging possibilities are compelling motives from which intuition cannot escape and to which all else must be sacrificed.

9. The Extraverted Intuitive Type

Whenever intuition predominates, a particular and unmistakable psychology presents itself. Because intuition is orientated by the object, a decided dependence upon external situations is discernible, but it has an altogether different character from the dependence of the sensational type. The intuitive is never to be found among the generally recognized reality values, but he is always present where possibilities exist. He has a keen nose for things in the bud pregnant with future promise. He can never exist in stable, long-established conditions of generally acknowledged though limited value: because his eye is constantly ranging for new possibilities, stable conditions have an air of impending suffocation. He seizes hold of new objects and new ways with eager intensity, sometimes with extraordinary enthusiasm, only to abandon them coldbloodedly, without regard and apparently without remembrance, as soon as their range becomes clearly defined and a promise of any considerable future development no longer clings to them. As long as a possibility exists, the intuitive is bound to it with thongs of fate. It is as though his whole life went out into the new situation. One gets the impression, which he himself shares, that he has just reached the definitive turning point in his life, and that from now on nothing else can seriously engage his thought and feeling. However reasonable and opportune it may be, and although every conceivable argument speaks in favour of stability, a day will come when nothing will deter him from regarding as a prison, the self-same situation that seemed to promise him freedom and deliverance, and from acting accordingly. Neither reason nor feeling can restrain or discourage him from a new possibility, even though it may run counter to convictions hitherto unquestioned. Thinking and feeling, the indispensable components of conviction, are, with him, inferior functions, possessing no decisive weight; hence they lack the power to offer any lasting. resistance to the force of intuition. And yet these are the only functions that are capable of creating any effectual compensation to the supremacy of intuition, since they can provide the intuitive with that *judgment* in which his type is altogether lacking. The morality of the intuitive is governed neither by intellect nor by feeling; he has his own characteristic morality, which consists in a loyalty to his intuitive view of things and a voluntary submission to its authority, Consideration for the welfare of his neighbours is weak. No solid argument hinges upon their well-being any more than upon his own. Neither can we detect in him any great respect for his neighbour's convictions and customs; in fact, he is not infrequently put down as an immoral and ruthless adventurer. Since his intuition is largely concerned with outer objects, scenting out external possibilities, he readily applies himself to callings wherein he may expand his abilities in many directions. Merchants, contractors, speculators, agents, politicians, etc., commonly belong to this type.

Apparently this type is more prone to favour women than men; in which case, however, the intuitive activity reveals itself not so much in the professional as in the social sphere. Such women understand the art of utilizing every social opportunity; they establish right social connections; they seek out lovers with possibilities only to abandon everything again for the sake of a new possibility.

It is at once clear, both from the standpoint of political economy and on grounds of general culture, that such a type is uncommonly important. If well-intentioned, with an orientation to life not purely egoistical, he may render exceptional service as the promoter, if not the initiator of every kind of promising enterprise. He is the natural advocate of every minority that holds the seed of future promise. Because of his capacity, when orientated more towards men than things, to make an intuitive diagnosis of their abilities and range of usefulness, he can also 'make' men. His capacity to inspire his fellow-men with courage, or to kindle enthusiasm for something new, is unrivalled, although he may have forsworn it by the morrow. The more powerful and vivid his intuition, the more is his subject fused and blended with the divined possibility. He animates it; he presents it in plastic shape and with convincing fire; he almost embodies it. It is not a mere histrionic display, but a fate.

This attitude has immense dangers -- all too easily the intuitive may squander his life. He spends himself animating men and things, spreading around him an abundance of life -- a life, however, which others live, not he. Were he able to rest with the actual thing, he would gather the fruit of his labours; yet all too soon must he be running after some fresh possibility, quitting his newly planted field, while others reap the harvest. In the end he goes empty away. But when the intuitive lets things reach such a pitch, he also has the unconscious against him. The unconscious of the intuitive has a certain similarity with that of the sensation-type. Thinking and feeling, being relatively repressed, produce infantile and archaic thoughts and feelings in the unconscious, which may be compared with those of the countertype. They likewise come to the surface in the form of intensive projections, and are just as absurd as those of the sensation-type, only to my mind they lack the other's mystical character; they are chiefly concerned with quasi-actual things, in the nature of sexual, financial, and other hazards, as, for instance, suspicions of approaching illness. This difference appears to be due to a repression of the sensations of actual things. These latter usually command attention in the shape of a sudden entanglement with a most unsuitable woman, or, in the case of a woman, with a thoroughly unsuitable man; and this is simply the result of their unwitting contact with the sphere of archaic sensations. But its consequence is an unconsciously compelling tie to an object of incontestable futility. Such an event is already a compulsive symptom, which is also thoroughly characteristic of this type. In common with the sensation-type, he claims a similar freedom and exemption from all restraint, since he suffers no submission of his decisions to rational judgment, relying entirely upon the perception of chance, possibilities. He rids himself of the restrictions of reason, only to fall a victim to unconscious neurotic compulsions in the form of oversubtle, negative reasoning, hair-splitting dialectics, and a compulsive tie to the sensation of the object. His conscious attitude, both to the sensation and the sensed object, is one of sovereign superiority and disregard. Not that he means to be inconsiderate or superior -- he simply does not see the object that everyone else sees; his oblivion is similar to that of the sensation-type -- only, with the latter, the soul of the object is missed. For this oblivion the object sooner or later takes revenge in the form of hypochondriacal, compulsive ideas, phobias, and every imaginable kind of absurd bodily sensation.

10. Recapitulation of Extraverted Irrational Types

I call the two preceding types *irrational* for reasons already referred to; namely, because their commissions and omissions are based not upon reasoned judgment but upon the absolute intensity of perception. Their perception is concerned with simple happenings, where no selection has been exercised by the judgment. In this respect both the latter types have a considerable superiority over the two judging types. The objective occurrence is both lawdetermined and accidental. In so far as it is law-determined, it is accessible to reason; in so far as it is accidental, it is not. One might reverse it and say that we apply the term law-determined to the occurrence appearing so to our reason, and where its regularity escapes us we call it accidental. The postulate of a universal lawfulness remains a postulate of reason only; in no sense is it a postulate of our functions of perception. Since these are in no way grounded upon the principle of reason and its postulates, they are, of their very nature, irrational. Hence my term 'irrational' corresponds with the nature of the perception-types. But merely because they subordinate judgment to perception, it would be quite incorrect to regard these types as unreasonable. They are merely in a high degree *empirical;* they are grounded exclusively upon experience, so exclusively, in fact, that as a rule, their judgment cannot keep pace with their experience. But the functions of judgment are none the less present, although they eke out a largely unconscious existence. But, since the unconscious, in spite of its separation from the conscious subject, is always reappearing on the scene, the actual life of the irrational types exhibits striking judgments and acts of choice, which take the form of apparent sophistries, coldhearted criticisms, and an apparently purposeful selection of persons and situations. These traits have a rather infantile, or even primitive, stamp; at times they are astonishingly naive, but at times also inconsiderate, crude, or outrageous. To the rationally orientated mind, the real character of such people might well appear rationalistic and purposeful in the bad sense. But this judgment would be valid only for their unconscious, and, therefore, quite incorrect for their conscious psychology, which is entirely orientated by perception, and because of its irrational nature is quite unintelligible to the rational judgment.

Finally, it may even appear to a rationally orientated mind that such an assemblage of accidentals, hardly deserves the name 'psychology.' The irrational type balances this contemptuous judgment with an equally poor impression of the rational; for he sees him as something only half alive, whose only aim in life consists in fastening the fetters of reason upon everything living, and wringing his own neck with criticisms. Naturally, these are gross extremes; but they occur.

From the standpoint of the rational type, the irrational might easily be represented as a rational of inferior quality; namely, when he is apprehended in the light of what happens to him. For what happens to him is not the accidental-in that he is master-but, in its stead, he is overtaken by rational judgment and rational aims. This fact is hardly comprehensible to the rational mind, but its unthinkableness merely equals the astonishment of the irrational, when he discovers someone who can set the ideas of reason above the living and actual event. Such a thing seems scarcely credible to him. It is, as a rule, quite hopeless to look to him for any recognition of principles in this direction, since a rational understanding is just as unknown and, in fact, tiresome to him as the idea of making a contract, without mutual discussion and obligations, appears unthinkable to the rational type.

This point brings me to the problem of the psychic relation between the representatives of the different types. Following the terminology of the French school of hypnotists, the psychic relation among the more modern psychiatrists is termed I 'rapport'. Rapport chiefly consists in a *feeling of actual accord,* in spite of recognised differences. In fact, the recognition of existing differences, in so far as they are common to both, is already a rapport, a feeling of accord. If we make this feeling conscious to a rather high degree in an actual case, we discover that it has not merely the quality of a feeling that cannot be analysed further, but it also has the nature of an insight or cognitional content, representing the point of agreement in a conceptual form. This rational presentation is exclusively valid for the rational types; it by no means applies to the irrational, whose rapport is based not at all upon judgment but upon the parallelism of actual living events. His feeling of accord is the common perception of a sensation or intuition. The rational would say that rapport with the irrational depends purely upon chance. If, by some accident, the objective situations are exactly in tune, something like a human relationship takes place, but nobody can tell what will be either its validity or its duration. To the rational type it is often a very bitter thought that the relationship will last only just so long as external circumstances accidentally produce a mutual interest. This does not occur to him as being especially human, whereas it is precisely in this situation that the irrational sees a humanity of quite singular beauty. Accordingly each regards the other as a man destitute of relationships, upon whom no reliance can be placed, and with whom one can never get on decent terms. Such a result, however, is reached only when one consciously tries to make some estimate of the nature of one's relationships with one's fellow-men. Although a psychological conscientiousness of this kind is by no means usual, yet it frequently happens that, notwithstanding an absolute difference of standpoint, a kind of rapport does take place, and in the following way. The one assumes with unspoken projection that the other is, in all essential points, of the same opinion as himself, while the other divines or senses an objective community of interest, of which, however, the former has no conscious inkling and whose existence he would at once dispute, just as it would never occur to the latter that his relationship must rest upon a common point-of-view. A rapport of this kind is by far the most frequent; it rests upon projection, which is the source of many subsequent misunderstandings.

Psychic relationship, in the extraverted attitude, is always regulated by objective factors and outer determinants. What a man is within has never any decisive significance. For our presentday culture the extraverted attitude is the governing principle in the problem of human relationship; naturally, the introverted principle occurs, but it is still the exception, and has to appeal to the tolerance of the age.

C. THE INTROVERTED TYPE

(I) *THE GENERAL ATTITUDE OF CONSCIOUSNESS*

As I have already explained in section A (1) of the present chapter, the introverted is distinguished from the extraverted type by the fact that, unlike the latter, who is prevailingly orientated by the object and objective data, he is governed by subjective factors. In the section alluded to I mentioned, inter alia, that the introvert interposes a subjective view between the perception of the object and his own action, which prevents the action from assuming a character that corresponds with the objective situation. Naturally, this is a special case, mentioned by way of example, and merely intended to serve as a simple illustration. But now we must go in quest of more general formulations.

Introverted consciousness doubtless views the external conditions, but it selects the subjective determinants as the decisive ones. The type is guided, therefore, by that factor of perception and cognition which represents the receiving subjective disposition to the sense stimulus. Two persons, for example, see the same object, but they never see it in such a way as to receive two identically similar images of it. Quite apart from the differences in the personal equation and mere organic acuteness, there often exists a radical difference, both in kind and degree, in the psychic assimilation of the perceived image. Whereas the extraverted type refers pre-eminently to that which reaches him from the object, the introvert principally relies upon that which the outer impression constellates [*sic*] in the subject. In an individual case of apperception, the difference may, of course, be very delicate, but in the total psychological economy it is extremely noticeable, especially in the form of a *reservation of the ego*. Although it is anticipating somewhat, I consider that point of view which inclines, with Weininger, to describe this attitude as philautic, or with other writers, as autoerotic, egocentric, subjective, or egoistic, to be both misleading in principle and definitely depreciatory. It corresponds with the normal bias of the extraverted attitude against the nature of the introvert. We must not forget-although extraverted opinion is only too prone to do so-that all perception and cognition is not purely objective: it is also subjectively conditioned. The world exists not merely in itself, but also as it appears to me. Indeed, at bottom, we have absolutely no criterion that could help us to form a judgment of a world whose nature was unassimilable by the subject. If we were to ignore the subjective factor, it would mean a complete denial of the great doubt as to the possibility of absolute cognition. And this would mean a rechute into that stale and hollow positivism which disfigured the beginning of our epoch -- an attitude of intellectual arrogance that is invariably accompanied by a crudeness of feeling, and an essential violation of life, as stupid as it is presumptuous. Through an overvaluation of the objective powers of cognition, we repress the importance of the subjective factor, which simply means the denial of the subject. But what is the subject? The subject is man -- we are the subject. Only a sick mind could forget that cognition must have a subject, for there exists no knowledge and, therefore, for us, no world where 'I know' has not been said, although with this statement one has already expressed the subjective limitation of all knowledge.

The same holds good for all the psychic functions: they have a subject which is just as indispensable as the object. It is characteristic of our present extraverted valuation that the word 'subjective' occasionally rings almost like a reproach or blemish; but in every case the epithet 'merely subjective' means a dangerous weapon of offence, destined for that daring head, that is not unceasingly convinced of the unconditioned superiority of the object. We must, therefore, be quite clear as to what meaning the term 'subjective' carries in this investigation. As the subjective factor, then, I understand that psychological action or reaction which, when merged with the effect of the object, makes a new psychic fact. Now, in so far as the subjective factor, since oldest times and among all peoples, remains in a very large measure identical with itself -- since elementary perceptions and cognitions are almost universally the same -- it is a reality that is just as firmly established as the outer object. If this were not so, any sort of permanent and essentially changeless would be altogether inconceivable, and any understanding with posterity would be a matter of impossibility. Thus far, therefore, the subjective factor is something that is just as much a fact as the extent of the sea and the radius of the earth. Thus far, also, the subjective factor claims the whole value of a world-determining power which can never, under any circumstances, be excluded from our calculations. It is the other world-law, and the man who is based upon it has a foundation just as secure, permanent, and valid, as the man who relies upon the object But, just as the object and objective data remain by no means always the same, inasmuch as they are both perishable and subject to chance, the subjective factor is similarly liable to variability and individual hazard. Hence its value is also merely relative. The excessive development of the introverted standpoint in consciousness, for instance, does not lead to a better or sounder application of the subjective factor, but to an artificial subjectification of consciousness, which can hardly escape the reproach 'merely subjective'. For, as a countertendency to this morbid subjectification, there ensues a desubjectification of consciousness in the form of an exaggerated extraverted attitude which richly deserves Weininger's description "misautic". Inasmuch as the introverted attitude is based upon a universally present, extremely real, and absolutely indispensable condition of psychological adaptation, such expressions as 'philautic', 'egocentric', and the like are both objectionable and out of place, since they foster the prejudice that it is invariably a question of the beloved ego. Nothing could be more absurd than such an assumption. Yet one is continually meeting it when examining the judgments of the extravert upon the introvert. Not, of course, that I wish to ascribe such an error to individual extraverts; it is rather the present generally accepted extraverted view which is by no means restricted to the extraverted type; for it finds just as many representatives in the ranks of the other type, albeit very much against its own interest. The reproach of being untrue to his own kind is justly levelled at the latter, whereas, this, at least, can never be charged against the former.

The introverted attitude is normally governed by the psychological structure, theoretically determined by heredity, but which to the subject is an ever present subjective factor. This must not be assumed, however, to be simply identical with the subject's ego, an assumption that is certainly implied in the above mentioned designations of Weininger; it is rather the psychological structure of the subject that precedes any development of the ego. The really fundamental subject, the Self, is far more comprehensive than the ego, because the former also embraces the unconscious, while the latter is essentially the focal point of consciousness. Were the ego identical with the Self, it would be unthinkable that we should be able to appear in dreams in entirely different forms and with entirely different meanings. But it is a characteristic peculiarity of the introvert, which, moreover, is as much in keeping with his own inclination as with the general bias, that he tends to confuse his ego with the Self, and to exalt his ego to the position of subject of the psychological process, thus effecting that morbid subjectification of consciousness, mentioned above, which so alienates him from the object.

The psychological structure is the same. Semon has termed it 'mneme' whereas I call it the *'collective unconscious'*. The individual Self is a portion, or excerpt, or representative, of something universally present in all living creatures, and, therefore, a correspondingly graduated kind of psychological process, which is born anew in every creature. Since earliest times, the inborn manner of *acting* has been called *instinct,* and for this manner of psychic apprehension of the object I have proposed the term *archetype.* I may assume that what is understood by instinct is familiar to everyone. It is another matter with the archetype. This term embraces the same idea as is contained in 'primordial image' (an expression borrowed from Jakob Burckhardt), and as such I have described it in Chapter xi of this book. I must here refer the reader to that chapter, in particular to the definition of 'image'.

The archetype is a symbolical formula, which always begins to function whenever there are no conscious ideas present, or when such as are present are impossible upon intrinsic or extrinsic grounds. The contents of the collective unconscious are represented in consciousness in the form of pronounced tendencies, or definite ways of looking at things. They are generally regarded by the individual as being determined by the object-incorrectly, at bottom-since they have their source in the unconscious structure of the psyche, and are only released by the operation of the object. These subjective tendencies and ideas are stronger than the objective influence; because their psychic value is higher, they are superimposed upon all impressions. Thus, just as it seems incomprehensible to the introvert that the object should always be decisive, it remains just as enigmatic to the extravert how a subjective standpoint can be superior to the objective situation. He reaches the unavoidable conclusion that the introvert is either a conceited egoist or a fantastic doctrinaire. Recently he seems to have reached the conclusion that the introvert is constantly influenced by an unconscious power-complex. The introvert unquestionably exposes himself to this prejudice; for it cannot be denied that his definite and highly generalized mode of expression, which apparently excludes every other view from the outset, lends a certain countenance to this extraverted opinion. Furthermore, the very decisiveness and inflexibility of the subjective judgment, which is superordinated to all objective data, is alone sufficient to create the impression of a strong egocentricity. The introvert usually lacks the right argument in presence of this prejudice; for he is just as unaware of the unconscious, though thoroughly sound presuppositions of his subjective judgment, as he is of his subjective perceptions. In harmony with the style of the times, he looks without, instead of behind his own consciousness for the answer. Should he become neurotic, it is the sign of a more or less complete unconscious identity of the ego with the Self, whereupon the importance of the Self is reduced to nil, while the ego becomes inflated beyond reason. The undeniable, worlddetermining power of the subjective factor then becomes concentrated in the ego, developing an immoderate power claim and a downright foolish egocentricity. Every psychology which reduces the nature of man to unconscious power instinct springs from this foundation. For example, Nietzsche's many faults in taste owe their existence to this subjectification of consciousness.

(II)   THE UNCONSCIOUS ATTITUDE

The superior position of the subjective factor in consciousness involves an inferiority of the objective factor. The object is not given that importance which should really belong to it. Just as it plays too great a role in the extraverted attitude, it has too little to say in the introverted. To the extent that the introvert's consciousness is subjectified, thus bestowing undue importance upon the ego, the object is placed in a position which in time becomes quite untenable. The object is a factor of undeniable power, while the ego is something very restricted and transitory. It would be a very different matter if the Self opposed the object. Self and world are commensurable factors; hence a normal introverted attitude is just as valid, and has as good a right to existence, as a normal extraverted attitude. But, if the ego has usurped the claims of the subject, a compensation naturally develops under the guise of an unconscious reinforcement of the influence of the object. Such a change eventually commands attention, for often, in spite of a positively convulsive attempt to ensure the superiority of the ego, the object and objective data develop an overwhelming influence, which is all the more invincible because it seizes upon the individual unawares, thus effecting an irresistible invasion of consciousness. As a result of the ego's defective relation to the object -- for a will to command is not adaptation -- a compensatory relation to the object develops in the unconscious, which makes itself felt in consciousness as an unconditional and irrepressible tie to the object. The more the ego seeks to secure every possible liberty, independence, superiority, and freedom from obligations, the deeper does it fall into the slavery of objective facts. The subject's freedom of mind is chained to an ignominious financial dependence, his unconcernedness of action suffers now and again, a distressing collapse in the face of public opinion, his moral superiority gets swamped in inferior relationships, and his desire to dominate ends in a pitiful craving to be loved. The chief concern of the unconscious in such a case is the relation to the object, and it affects this in a way that is calculated to bring both the power illusion and the superiority phantasy to utter ruin. The object assumes terrifying dimensions, in spite of conscious depreciation. Detachment from, and command of, the object are, in consequence, pursued by the ego still more violently. Finally, the ego surrounds itself by a regular system of safeguards (Adler has ably depicted these) which shall at least preserve the illusion of superiority. But, therewith, the introvert severs himself completely from the object, and either squanders his energy in defensive measures or makes fruitless attempts to impose his power upon the object and successfully assert himself. But these efforts are constantly being frustrated by the overwhelming impressions he receives from the object. It continually imposes itself upon him against his will; it provokes in him the most disagreeable and obstinate affects, persecuting him at every step. An immense, inner struggle is constantly required of him, in order to 'keep going.' Hence *Psychoasthenia* is his typical form of neurosis, a malady which is characterized on the one hand by an extreme sensitiveness, and on the other by a great liability to exhaustion and chronic fatigue.

An analysis of the personal unconscious yields an abundance of power phantasies coupled with fear of the dangerously animated objects, to which, as a matter of fact, the introvert easily falls a victim. For a peculiar cowardliness develops from this fear of the object; he shrinks from making either himself or his opinion effective, always dreading an intensified influence on the part of the object. He is terrified of impressive affects in others, and is hardly ever free from the dread of falling under hostile influence. For objects possess terrifying and powerful qualities for himqualities which he cannot consciously discern in them, but which, through his unconscious perception, he cannot choose but believe in.

Since his conscious relation to the object is relatively repressed, its exit is by way of the unconscious, where it becomes loaded with the qualities of the unconscious. These qualities are primarily infantile and archaic. His relation to the object, therefore, becomes correspondingly primitive, taking on all those peculiarities which characterize the primitive objectrelationship. Now it seems as though objects possessed magical powers. Strange, new objects excite fear and distrust, as though concealing unknown dangers; objects long rooted and blessed by tradition are attached to his soul as by invisible threads; every change has a disturbing, if not actually dangerous aspect, since its apparent implication is a magical animation of the object. A lonely island where only what is permitted to move moves, becomes an ideal. *Auch Einer,* the novel by F. Th. Vischer, gives a rich insight into this side of the introvert's psychology, and at the same time shows the underlying symbolism of the collective unconscious, which in this description of types I am leaving on one side, since it is a universal phenomenon with no especial connection with types.

(III) PECULIARITIES OF THE BASIC PSYCHOLOGICAL FUNCTIONS IN THE INTROVERTED ATTITUDE

1. Thinking

When describing extraverted thinking, I gave a brief characterization of introverted thinking, to which at this stage I must make further reference. Introverted thinking is primarily orientated by the subjective factor. At the least, this subjective factor is represented by a subjective feeling of direction, which, in the last resort, determines judgment. Occasionally, it is a more or less finished image, which to some extent, serves as a standard. This thinking may be conceived either with concrete or with abstract factors, but always at the decisive points it is orientated by subjective data. Hence, it does not lead from concrete experience back again into objective things, but always to the subjective content, External facts are not the aim and origin of this thinking, although the introvert would often like to make it so appear. It begins in the subject, and returns to the subject, although it may undertake the widest flights into the territory of the real and the actual. Hence, in the statement of new facts, its chief value is indirect, because new views rather than the perception of new facts are its main concern. It formulates questions and creates theories; it opens up prospects and yields insight, but in the presence of facts it exhibits a reserved demeanour. As illustrative examples they have their value, but they must not prevail. Facts are collected as evidence or examples for a theory, but never for their own sake. Should this latter ever occur, it is done only as a compliment to the extraverted style. For this kind of thinking facts are of secondary importance; what, apparently, is of absolutely paramount importance is the development and presentation of the subjective idea, that primordial symbolical image standing more or less darkly before the inner vision. Its aim, therefore, is never concerned with an intellectual reconstruction of concrete actuality, but with the shaping of that dim image into a resplendent idea. Its desire is to reach reality; its goal is to see how external facts fit into, and fulfil, the framework of the idea; its actual creative power is proved by the fact that this thinking can also create that idea which, though not present in the external facts, is yet the most suitable, abstract expression of them. Its task is accomplished when the idea it has fashioned seems to emerge so inevitably from the external facts that they actually prove its validity.

But just as little as it is given to extraverted thinking to wrest a really sound inductive idea from concrete facts or ever to create new ones, does it lie in the power of introverted thinking to translate its original image into an idea adequately adapted to the facts. For, as in the former case the purely empirical heaping together of facts paralyses thought and smothers their meaning, so in the latter case introverted thinking shows a dangerous tendency to coerce facts into the shape of its image, or by ignoring them altogether, to unfold its phantasy image in freedom. In such a case, it will be impossible for the presented idea to deny its origin from the dim archaic image. There will cling to it a certain mythological character that we are prone to interpret as 'originality', or in more pronounced cases' as mere whimsicality; since its archaic character is not transparent as such to specialists unfamiliar with mythological motives. The subjective force of conviction inherent in such an idea is usually very great; its power too is the more convincing, the less it is influenced by contact with outer facts. Although to the man who advocates the idea, it may well seem that his scanty store of facts were the actual ground and source of the truth and validity of his idea, yet such is not the case, for the idea derives its convincing power from its unconscious archetype, which, as such, has universal validity and everlasting truth. Its truth, however, is so universal and symbolic, that it must first enter into the recognized and recognizable knowledge of the time, before it can become a practical truth of any real value to life. What sort of a causality would it be, for instance, that never became perceptible in practical causes and practical results?

This thinking easily loses itself in the immense truth of the subjective factor. It creates theories for the sake of theories, apparently with a view to real or at least possible facts, yet always with a distinct tendency to go over from the world of ideas into mere imagery. Accordingly many intuitions of possibilities appear on the scene, none of which however achieve any reality, until finally images are produced which no longer express anything externally real, being 'merely' symbols of the simply unknowable. It is now merely a mystical thinking and quite as unfruitful as that empirical thinking whose sole operation is within the framework of objective facts.

Whereas the latter sinks to the level of a mere presentation of facts, the former evaporates into a representation of the unknowable, which is even beyond everything that could be expressed in an image. The presentation of facts has a certain incontestable truth, because the subjective factor is excluded and the facts speak for themselves. Similarly, the representing of the unknowable has also an immediate, subjective, and convincing power, because it is demonstrable from its own existence. The former says 'Est, ergo est' ('It is ; therefore it is') ; while the latter says 'Cogito, ergo cogito' (' I think ; therefore I think'). In the last analysis, introverted thinking arrives at the evidence of its own subjective being, while extraverted thinking is driven to the evidence of its complete identity with the objective fact. For, while the extravert really denies himself in his complete dispersion among objects, the introvert, by ridding himself of each and every content, has to content himself with his mere existence. In both cases the further development of life is crowded out of the domain of thought into the region of other psychic functions which had hitherto existed in relative unconsciousness. The extraordinary impoverishment of introverted thinking in relation to objective facts finds compensation in an abundance of unconscious facts. Whenever consciousness, wedded to the function of thought, confines itself within the smallest and emptiest circle possible -- though seeming to contain the plenitude of divinity -- unconscious phantasy becomes proportionately enriched by a multitude of archaically formed facts, a veritable pandemonium of magical and irrational factors, wearing the particular aspect that accords with the nature of that function which shall next relieve the thought-function as the representative of life. If this should be the intuitive function, the 'other side' will be viewed with the eyes of a Kubin or a Meyrink. If it is the feeling-function, there arise quite unheard of and fantastic feeling-relations, coupled with feeling-judgments of a quite contradictory and unintelligible character. If the sensation-function, then the senses discover some new and neverbefore-experienced possibility, both within and without the body. A closer investigation of such changes can easily demonstrate the reappearance of primitive psychology with all its characteristic features. Naturally, the thing experienced is not merely primitive but also symbolic; in fact, the older and more primeval it appears, the more does it represent the future truth: since everything ancient in our unconscious means the coming possibility.

Under ordinary circumstances, not even the transition to the 'other side' succeeds -- still less the redeeming journey through the unconscious. The passage across is chiefly prevented by conscious resistance to any subjection of the ego to the unconscious reality and to the determining reality of the unconscious object. The condition is a dissociation-in other words, a neurosis having the character of an inner wastage with increasing brain-exhaustion -- a psychoasthenia, in fact.

2. The Introverted Thinking Type

Just as Darwin might possibly represent the normal extraverted thinking type, so we might point to Kant as a counter-example of the normal introverted thinking type. The former speaks with facts; the latter appeals to the subjective factor. Darwin ranges over the wide fields of objective facts, while Kant restricts himself to a critique of knowledge in general. But suppose a Cuvier be contrasted with a Nietzsche: the antithesis becomes even sharper.

The introverted thinking type is characterized by a priority of the thinking I have just described. Like his extraverted parallel, he is decisively influenced by ideas; these, however, have their origin, not in the objective data but in the subjective foundation. Like the extravert, he too will follow his ideas, but in the reverse direction: inwardly not outwardly. Intensity is his aim,

not extensity. In these fundamental characters he differs markedly, indeed quite unmistakably from his extraverted parallel. Like every introverted type, he is almost completely lacking in that which distinguishes his counter type, namely, the intensive relatedness to the object. In the case of a human object, the man has a distinct feeling that he matters only in a negative way, *i.e.,* in milder instances he is merely conscious of being superfluous, but with a more extreme type he feels himself warded off as something definitely disturbing. This negative relation to the objectindifference, and even aversion-characterizes every introvert; it also makes a description of the introverted type in general extremely difficult. With him, everything tends to disappear and get concealed. His judgment appears cold, obstinate, arbitrary, and inconsiderate, simply because he is related less to the object than the subject. One can feel nothing in it that might possibly confer a higher value upon the object; it always seems to go beyond the object, leaving behind it a flavour of a certain subjective superiority. Courtesy, amiability, and friendliness may be present, but often with a particular quality suggesting a certain uneasiness, which betrays an ulterior aim, namely, the disarming of an opponent, who must at all costs be pacified and set at ease lest he prove a disturbing- element. In no sense, of course, is he an opponent, but, if at all sensitive, he will feel somewhat repelled, perhaps even depreciated. Invariably the object has to submit to a certain neglect; in worse cases it is even surrounded with quite unnecessary measures of precaution. Thus it happens that this type tends to disappear behind a cloud of misunderstanding, which only thickens the more he attempts to assume, by way of compensation and with the help of his inferior functions, a certain mask of urbanity, which often presents a most vivid contrast to his real nature. Although in the extension of his world of ideas he shrinks from no risk, however daring, and never even considers the possibility that such a world might also be dangerous, revolutionary, heretical, and wounding to feeling, he is none the less a prey to the liveliest anxiety, should it ever chance to become objectively real. That goes against the grain. When the time comes for him to transplant his ideas into the world, his is by no means the air of an anxious mother solicitous for her children's welfare; he merely exposes them, and is often extremely annoyed when they fail to thrive on their own account. The decided lack he usually displays in practical ability, and his aversion from any sort of re[accent]clame assist in this attitude. If to his eyes his product appears subjectively correct and true, it must also be so in practice, and others have simply got to bow to its truth. Hardly ever will he go out of his way to win anyone's appreciation of it, especially if it be anyone of influence. And, when he brings himself to do so, he is usually so extremely maladroit that he merely achieves the opposite of his purpose. In his own special province, there are usually awkward experiences with his colleagues, since he never knows how to win their favour; as a rule he only succeeds in showing them how entirely superfluous they are to him. In the pursuit of his ideas he is generally stubborn, head-strong, and quite unamenable to influence.

His suggestibility to personal influences is in strange contrast to this. An object has only to be recognized as apparently innocuous for such a type to become extremely accessible to really inferior elements. They lay hold of him from the unconscious. He lets himself be brutalized and exploited in the most ignominious way, if only he can be left undisturbed in the pursuit of his ideas. He simply does not see when he is being plundered behind his back and wronged in practical ways: this is because his relation to the object is such a secondary matter that lie is left without a guide in the purely objective valuation of his product. In thinking out his problems to the utmost of his ability, he also complicates them, and constantly becomes entangled in every possible scruple. However clear to himself the inner structure of his thoughts may be, he is not in the least clear where and how they link up with the world of reality. Only with difficulty can he persuade himself to admit that what is clear to him may not be equally clear to everyone. His style is usually loaded and complicated by all sorts of accessories, qualifications, saving clauses, doubts, etc., which spring from his exacting scrupulousness. His work goes slowly and with difficulty. Either he is taciturn or he falls among people who cannot understand him; whereupon he proceeds to gather further proof of the unfathomable stupidity of man. If he should ever chance to be understood, he is credulously liable to overestimate. Ambitious women have only to understand how advantage may be taken of his uncritical attitude towards the object to make an easy prey of him; or he may develop into a misanthropic bachelor with a childlike heart. Then, too, his outward appearance is often gauche, as if he were painfully anxious to escape observation; or he may show a remarkable unconcern, an almost childlike naivete. In his own particular field of work he provokes violent contradiction, with which he has no notion how to deal, unless by chance he is seduced by his primitive affects into biting and fruitless polemics. By his wider circle he is counted inconsiderate and domineering. But the better one knows him, the more favourable one's judgment becomes, and his nearest friends are well aware how to value his intimacy. To people who judge him from afar he appears prickly, inaccessible, haughty; frequently he may even seem soured as a result of his anti-social prejudices. He has little influence as a personal teacher, since the mentality of his pupils is strange to him. Besides, teaching has, at bottom, little interest for him, except when it accidentally provides him with a theoretical problem. He is a poor teacher, because while teaching his thought is engaged with the actual material, and will not be satisfied with its mere presentation.

With the intensification of his type, his convictions become all the more rigid and unbending. Foreign influences are eliminated; he becomes more unsympathetic to his peripheral world, and therefore more dependent upon his intimates. His expression becomes more personal and inconsiderate and his ideas more profound, but they can no longer be adequately expressed in the material at hand. This lack is replaced by emotivity and susceptibility. The foreign influence, brusquely declined from without, reaches him from within, from the side of the unconscious, and he is obliged to collect evidence against it and against things in general which to outsiders seems quite superfluous. Through the subjectification of consciousness occasioned by his defective relationship to the object, what secretly concerns his own *person* now seems to him of chief importance. And he begins to confound his subjective truth with his own person. Not that he will attempt to press anyone personally with his convictions, but he will break out with venomous and personal retorts against every criticism, however just. Thus in every respect his isolation gradually increases. His originally fertilizing ideas become destructive, because poisoned by a kind of sediment of bitterness. His struggle against the influences emanating [p. 489] from the unconscious increases with his external isolation, until gradually this begins to cripple him. A still greater isolation must surely protect him from the unconscious influences, but as a rule this only takes him deeper into the conflict which is destroying him within.

The thinking of the introverted type is positive and synthetic in the development of those ideas which in ever increasing measure approach the eternal validity of the primordial images. But, when their connection with objective experience begins to fade, they become mythological and untrue for the present situation. Hence this thinking holds value only for its contemporaries, just so long as it also stands in visible and understandable connection with the known facts of the time. But, when thinking becomes mythological, its irrelevancy grows until finally it gets lost in itself. The relatively unconscious functions of feeling, intuition, and sensation, which counterbalance introverted thinking, are inferior in quality and have a primitive, extraverted character, to which all the troublesome objective influences this type is subject to must be ascribed. The various measures of self-defence, the curious protective obstacles with which such people are wont to surround themselves, are sufficiently familiar, and I may, therefore, spare myself a description of them. They all serve as a defence against 'magical' influences; a vague dread of the other sex also belongs to this category.

3. Feeling

Introverted feeling is determined principally by the subjective factor. This means that the feelingjudgment differs quite as essentially from extraverted feeling as does the introversion of thinking from extraversion. It is unquestionably difficult to give an intellectual presentation of the introverted feeling process, or even an approximate description of it, although the peculiar character of this kind of feeling simply stands out as soon as one becomes aware of it at all. Since it is primarily controlled by subjective preconditions, and is only secondarily concerned with the object, this feeling appears much less upon the surface and is, as a rule, misunderstood. It is a feeling which apparently depreciates the object; hence it usually becomes noticeable in its negative manifestations. The existence of a positive feeling can be inferred only indirectly, as it were. Its aim is not so much to accommodate to the objective fact as to stand above it, since its whole unconscious effort is to give reality to the underlying images. It is, as it were, continually seeking an image which has no existence in reality, but of which it has had a sort of previous vision. From objects that can never fit in with its aim it seems to glide unheedingly away. It strives after an inner intensity, to which at the most, objects contribute only an accessory stimulus. The depths of this feeling can only be divined -- they can never be clearly comprehended. It makes men silent and difficult of access; with the sensitiveness of the mimosa, it shrinks from the brutality of the object, in order to expand into the depths of the subject. It puts forward negative feeling-judgments or assumes an air of profound indifference, as a measure of self-defence.

Primordial images are, of course, just as much idea as feeling. Thus, basic ideas such as God, freedom, immortality are just as much feeling-values as they are significant as ideas. Everything, therefore, that has been said of the introverted thinking refers equally to introverted feeling, only here everything is felt while there it was thought. But the fact that thoughts can generally be expressed more intelligibly than feelings demands a more than ordinary descriptive or artistic capacity before the real wealth of this feeling can be even approximately presented or communicated to the outer world. Whereas subjective thinking, on account of its unrelatedness, finds great difficulty in arousing an adequate understanding, the same, though in perhaps even higher degree, holds good for subjective feeling. In order to communicate with others it has to find an external form which is not only fitted to absorb the subjective feeling in a satisfying expression, but which must also convey it to one's fellowman in such a way that a parallel process takes place in him. Thanks to the relatively great internal (as well as external) similarity of the human being, this effect can actually be achieved, although a form acceptable to feeling is extremely difficult to find, so long as it is still mainly orientated by the fathomless store of primordial images. But, when it becomes falsified by an egocentric attitude, it at once grows unsympathetic, since then its major concern is still with the ego. Such a case never fails to create an impression of sentimental self-love, with its constant effort to arouse interest and even morbid self-admiration just as the subjectified consciousness of the introverted thinker, striving after an abstraction of abstractions, only attains a supreme intensity of a thought-process in itself quite empty, so the intensification of egocentric feeling only leads to a contentless passionateness, which merely feels itself. This is the mystical, ecstatic stage, which prepares the way over into the extraverted functions repressed by feeling, just as introverted thinking is pitted against a primitive feeling, to which objects attach themselves with magical force, so introverted feeling is counterbalanced by a primitive thinking, whose concretism and slavery to facts passes all bounds. Continually emancipating itself from the relation to the object, this feeling creates a freedom, both of action and of conscience, that is only answerable to the subject, and that may even renounce all traditional values. But so much the more does unconscious thinking fall a victim to the power of objective facts.

4. The Introverted Feeling Type

It is principally among women that I have found the priority of introverted feeling. The proverb 'Still waters run deep' is very true of such women. They are mostly silent, inaccessible, and hard to understand; often they hide behind a childish or banal mask, and not infrequently their temperament is melancholic. They neither shine nor reveal themselves. Since they submit the control of their lives to their subjectively orientated feeling, their true motives generally remain concealed. Their outward demeanour is harmonious and inconspicuous; they reveal a delightful repose, a sympathetic parallelism, which has no desire to affect others, either to impress, influence, or change them in any way. Should this outer side be somewhat emphasized, a suspicion of neglectfulness and coldness may easily obtrude itself, which not seldom increases to a real indifference for the comfort and well-being of others. One distinctly feels the movement of feeling away from the object. With the normal type, however, such an event only occurs when the object has in some way too strong an effect. The harmonious feeling atmosphere rules only so long as the object moves upon its own way with a moderate feeling intensity, and makes no attempt to cross the other's path. There is little effort to accompany the real emotions of the object, which tend to be damped and rebuffed, or to put it more aptly, are 'cooled off' by a negative feeling-judgment. Although one may find a constant readiness for a peaceful and harmonious companionship, the unfamiliar object is shown no touch of amiability, no gleam of responding warmth, but is met by a manner of apparent indifference or repelling coldness. One may even be made to feel the superfluousness of one's own existence. In the presence of something that might carry one away or arouse enthusiasm, this type observes a benevolent neutrality, tempered with an occasional trace of superiority and criticism that soon takes the wind out of the sails of a sensitive object. But a stormy emotion will be brusquely rejected with murderous coldness, unless it happens to catch the subject from the side of the unconscious, *i.e.* unless, through the animation of some primordial image, feeling is, as it were, taken captive. In which event such a woman simply feels a momentary laming, invariably producing, in due course, a still more violent resistance, which reaches the object in his most vulnerable spot. The relation to the object is, as far as possible, kept in a secure and tranquil middle state of feeling, where passion and its intemperateness are resolutely proscribed. Expression of feeling, therefore, remains niggardly and, when once aware of it at all, the object has a permanent sense of his undervaluation. Such, however, is not always the case, since very often the deficit remains unconscious; whereupon the unconscious feeling-claims gradually produce symptoms which compel a more serious attention.

A superficial judgment might well be betrayed, by a rather cold and reserved demeanour, into denying all feeling to this type. Such a view, however, would be quite false; the truth is, her feelings are intensive rather than extensive. They develop into the depth. Whereas, for instance, an extensive feeling of sympathy can express itself in both word and deed at the right place, thus quickly ridding itself of its impression, an intensive sympathy, because shut off from every means of expression, gains a passionate depth that embraces the misery of a world and is simply benumbed. It may possibly make an extravagant irruption, leading to some staggering act of an almost heroic character, to which, however, neither the object nor the subject can find a right relation. To the outer world, or to the blind eyes of the extravert, this sympathy looks like coldness, for it does nothing visibly, and an extraverted consciousness is unable to believe in invisible forces.

Such misunderstanding is a characteristic occurrence in the life of this type, and is commonly registered as a most weighty argument against any deeper feeling relation with the object. But the underlying, real object of this feeling is only dimly divined by the normal type. It may possibly express its aim and content in a concealed religiosity anxiously shielded, from profane eyes, or in intimate poetic forms equally safeguarded from surprise; not without a secret ambition to bring about some superiority over the object by such means. Women often express much of it in their children, letting their passionateness flow secretly into them.

Although in the normal type, the tendency, above alluded to, to overpower or coerce the object once openly and visibly with the thing secretly felt, rarely plays a disturbing role, and never leads to a serious attempt in this direction, some trace of it, none the less, leaks through into the personal effect upon the object, in the form of a domineering influence often difficult to define. It is sensed as a sort of stifling or oppressive feeling which holds the immediate circle under a spell. It gives a woman of this type a certain mysterious power that may prove terribly fascinating to the extraverted man, for it touches his unconscious. This power is derived from the deeply felt, unconscious images; consciousness, however, readily refers it to the ego, whereupon the influence becomes debased into personal tyranny. But, wherever the unconscious subject is identified with the ego, the mysterious power of the intensive feeling is also transformed into banal and arrogant ambition, vanity, and petty tyranny. This produces a type of woman most regrettably distinguished by her unscrupulous ambition and mischievous cruelty. But this change in the picture leads also to neurosis.

So long as the ego feels itself housed, as it were, beneath the heights of the unconscious subject, and feeling reveals something higher and mightier than the ego, the type is normal. The unconscious thinking is certainly archaic, yet its reductions may prove extremely helpful in compensating the occasional inclinations to exalt the ego into the subject. But, whenever this does take place by dint of complete suppression of the unconscious reductive thinking-products, the unconscious thinking goes over into opposition and becomes projected into objects. Whereupon the now egocentric subject comes to feel the power and importance of the depreciated object. Consciousness begins to feel 'what others think'. Naturally, others are thinking, all sorts of baseness, scheming evil, and contriving all sorts of plots, secret intrigues, etc. To prevent this, the subject must also begin to carry out preventive intrigues, to suspect and sound others, to make subtle combinations. Assailed by rumours, he must make convulsive efforts to convert, if possible, a threatened inferiority into a superiority. Innumerable secret rivalries develop, and in these embittered struggles not only will no base or evil means be disdained, but even virtues will be misused and tampered with in order to play the trump card. Such a development must lead to exhaustion. The form of neurosis is neurasthenic rather than hysterical; in the case of women we often find severe collateral physical states, as for instance anæmia and its sequelæ.

5. Recapitulation of Introverted Rational Types

Both the foregoing types are rational, since they are founded upon reasoning, judging functions.

Reasoning judgment is based not merely upon objective, but also upon subjective, data. But the predominance of one or other factor, conditioned by a psychic disposition often existing from early youth, deflects the reasoning function. For a judgment to be really reasonable it should have equal reference to both the objective and the subjective factors, and be able to do justice to both. This, however, would be an ideal case, and would presuppose a uniform development of both extraversion and introversion. But either movement excludes the other, and, so long as this dilemma persists, they cannot possibly exist side by, side, but at the most successively. Under ordinary circumstances, therefore, an ideal reason is impossible. A rational type has always a typical reasonal variation. Thus, the introverted rational types unquestionably have a reasoning judgment, only it is a judgment whose leading note is subjective. The laws of logic are not necessarily deflected, since its onesidedness lies in the premise. The premise is the predominance of the subjective factor existing beneath every conclusion and colouring every judgment. Its superior value as compared with the objective factor is self-evident from the beginning. As already stated, it is not just a question of value bestowed, but of a natural disposition existing before all rational valuation. Hence, to the introvert rational judgment necessarily appears to have many nuances which differentiate it from that of the extravert. Thus, to the introvert, to mention the most general instance, that chain of reasoning which leads to the subjective factor appears rather more reasonable than that which leads to the object. This difference, which in the individual case is practically insignificant, indeed almost unnoticeable, effects unbridgeable oppositions in the gross; these are the more irritating, the less we are aware of the minimal standpoint displacement produced by the psychological premise in the individual case. A [p. 497] capital error regularly creeps in here, for one labours to prove a fallacy in the conclusion, instead of realizing the difference of the psychological premise. Such a realization is a difficult matter for every rational type, since it undermines the apparent, absolute validity of his own principle, and delivers him over to its antithesis, which certainly amounts to a catastrophe.

Almost more even than the extraverted is the introverted type subject to misunderstanding: not so much because the extravert is a more merciless or critical adversary, than he himself can easily be, but because the style of the epoch in which he himself participates is against him. Not in relation to the extraverted type, but as against our general accidental world-philosophy, he finds himself in the minority, not of course numerically, but from the evidence of his own feeling. In so far as he is a convinced participator in the general style, he undermines his own foundations, since the present style, with its almost exclusive acknowledgment of the visible and the tangible, is opposed to his principle. Because of its invisibility, he is obliged to depreciate the subjective factor, and to force himself to join in the extraverted overvaluation of the object. He himself sets the subjective factor at too low a value, and his feelings of inferiority are his chastisement for this sin. Little wonder, therefore, that it is precisely our epoch, and particularly those movements which are somewhat ahead of the time, that reveal the subjective factor in every kind of exaggerated, crude and grotesque form of expression. I refer to the art of the present day.

The undervaluation of his own principle makes the introvert egotistical, and forces upon him the psychology of the oppressed. The more egotistical he becomes, the stronger his impression grows that these others, who are apparently able, without qualms, to conform with the present style, are the oppressors against whom he must guard and protect himself. He does not usually perceive that he commits his capital mistake in not depending upon the subjective factor with that same loyalty and devotion with which the extravert follows the object By the undervaluation of his own principle, his penchant towards egoism becomes unavoidable, which, of course, richly deserves the prejudice of the extravert. Were he only to remain true to his own principle, the judgment of 'egoist' would be radically false; for the justification of his attitude would be established by its general efficacy, and all misunderstandings dissipated.

6. Sensation

Sensation, which in obedience to its whole nature is concerned with the object and the objective stimulus, also undergoes a considerable modification in the introverted attitude. It, too, has a subjective factor, for beside the object sensed there stands a sensing subject, who contributes his subjective disposition to the objective stimulus. In the introverted attitude sensation is definitely based upon the subjective portion of perception. What is meant by this finds its best illustration in the reproduction of objects in art. When, for instance, several painters undertake to paint one and the same landscape, with a sincere attempt to reproduce it faithfully, each painting will none the less differ from the rest, not merely by virtue of a more or less developed ability, but chiefly because of a different vision; there will even appear in some of the paintings a decided psychic variation, both in general mood and in treatment of colour and form. Such qualities betray a more or less influential co-operation of the subjective factor. The subjective factor of sensation is essentially the same as in the other functions already spoken of. It is an unconscious disposition, which alters the sense-perception at its very source, thus depriving it of the character of a purely objective influence. In this case, sensation is related primarily to the subject, and only secondarily to the object. How extraordinarily strong the subjective factor can be is shown most clearly in art. The ascendancy of the subjective factor occasionally achieves a complete suppression of the mere influence of the object; but none the less sensation remains sensation, although it has come to be a perception of the subjective factor, and the effect of the object has sunk to the level of a mere stimulant. Introverted sensation develops in accordance with this subjective direction. A true sense-perception certainly exists, but it always looks as though objects were not so much forcing their way into the subject in their own right as that the subject were seeing things quite differently, or saw quite other things than the rest of mankind. As a matter of fact, the subject perceives the same things as everybody else, only, he never stops at the purely objective effect, but concerns himself with the subjective perception released by the objective stimulus. Subjective perception differs remarkably from the objective. It is either not found at all in the object, or, at most, merely suggested by it; it can, however, be similar to the sensation of other men, although not immediately derived from the objective behaviour of things. It does not impress one as a mere product of consciousness -- it is too genuine for that. But it makes a definite psychic impression, since elements of a higher psychic order are perceptible to it. This order, however, does not coincide with the contents of consciousness. It is concerned with presuppositions, or dispositions of the collective unconscious, with mythological images, with primal possibilities of ideas. The character of significance and meaning clings to subjective perception. It says more than the mere image of the object, though naturally only to him for whom the subjective factor has some meaning. To another, a reproduced subjective impression seems to suffer from the defect of possessing insufficient similarity with the object; it seems, therefore, to have failed in its purpose. Subjective sensation apprehends the background of the physical world rather than its surface. The decisive thing is not the reality of the object, but the reality of the subjective factor, *i.e.* the primordial images, which in their totality represent a psychic mirror-world. It is a mirror, however, with the peculiar capacity of representing the present contents of consciousness not in their known and customary form but in a certain sense sub specie aeternitatis, somewhat as a million-year old consciousness might see them. Such a consciousness would see the becoming and the passing of things beside their present and momentary existence, and not only that, but at the same time it would also see that Other, which was before their becoming and will be after their passing hence. To this consciousness the present moment is improbable. This is, of course, only a simile, of which, however, I had need to give some sort of illustration of the peculiar nature of introverted sensation. Introverted sensation conveys an image whose effect is not so much to reproduce the object as to throw over it a wrapping whose lustre is derived from age-old subjective experience and the still unborn future event. Thus, mere sense impression develops into the depth of the meaningful, while extraverted sensation seizes only the momentary and manifest existence of things.

7. The Introverted Sensation Type

The priority of introverted sensation produces a definite type, which is characterized by certain peculiarities. It is an irrational type, inasmuch as its selection among occurrences is not primarily rational, but is guided rather by what just happens. Whereas, the extraverted sensationtype is determined by the intensity of the objective influence, the introverted type is orientated by the intensity of the subjective sensation-constituent released by the objective stimulus. Obviously, therefore, no sort of proportional relation exists between object and sensation, but something that is apparently quite irregular and arbitrary judging from without, therefore, it is practically impossible to foretell what will make an impression and what will not. If there were present a capacity and readiness for expression in any way commensurate with the strength of sensation, the irrationality of this type would be extremely evident. This is the case, for instance, when the individual is a creative artist. But, since this is the exception, it usually happens that the characteristic introverted difficulty of expression also conceals his irrationality. On the contrary, he may actually stand out by the very calmness and passivity of his demeanour, or by his rational self-control. This peculiarity, which often leads the superficial judgment astray, is really due to his unrelatedness to objects. Normally the object is not consciously depreciated in the least, but its stimulus is removed from it, because it is immediately replaced by a subjective reaction, which is no longer related to the reality of the object. This, of course, has the same effect as a depreciation of the object. Such a type can easily make one question why one should exist at all; or why objects in general should have any right to existence, since everything essential happens without the object. This doubt may be justified in extreme cases, though not in the normal, since the objective stimulus is indispensable to his sensation, only it produces something different from what was to be surmised from the external state of affairs. Considered from without, it looks as though the effect of the object did not obtrude itself upon the subject. This impression is so far correct inasmuch as a subjective content does, in fact, intervene from the unconscious, thus snatching away the effect of the object. This intervention may be so abrupt that the individual appears to shield himself directly from any possible influence of the object. In any aggravated or well-marked case, such a protective guard is also actually present. Even with only a slight reinforcement of the unconscious, the subjective constituent of sensation becomes so alive that it almost completely obscures the objective influence. The results of this are, on the one hand, a feeling of complete depreciation on the part of the object, and, on the other, an illusory conception of reality on the part of the subject, which in morbid cases may even reach the point of a complete inability to discriminate between the real object and the subjective perception. Although so vital a distinction vanishes completely only in a practically psychotic state, yet long before that point is reached subjective perception may influence thought, feeling, and action to an extreme degree, in spite of the fact that the object is clearly seen in its fullest reality. Whenever the objective influence does succeed in forcing its way into the subject -- as the result of particular circumstances of special intensity, or because of a more perfect analogy with the unconscious image -- even the normal example of this type is induced to *act* in accordance with his unconscious model. Such action has an illusory quality in relation to objective reality, and therefore has a very odd

and strange character. It instantly reveals the antireal subjectivity of the type, But, where the influence of the object does not entirely succeed, it encounters a benevolent neutrality, disclosing little sympathy, yet constantly striving to reassure and adjust. The too-low is raised a little, the too-high is made a little lower; the enthusiastic is damped, the extravagant restrained; and the unusual brought within the 'correct' formula: all this in order to keep the influence of the object within the necessary bounds. Thus, this type becomes an affliction to his circle, just in so far as his entire harmlessness is no longer above suspicion. But, if the latter should be the case, the individual readily becomes a victim to the aggressiveness and ambitions of others. Such men allow themselves to be abused, for which they usually take vengeance at the most unsuitable occasions with redoubled stubbornness and resistance. When there exists no capacity for artistic expression, all impressions sink into the inner depths, whence they hold consciousness under a spell, removing any possibility it might have had of mastering the fascinating impression by means of conscious expression. Relatively
speaking, this type has only archaic possibilities of expression for the disposal of his impressions; thought and feeling are relatively unconscious, and, in so far as they have a certain consciousness, they only serve in the necessary, banal, every-day expressions. Hence as conscious functions, they are wholly unfitted to give any adequate rendering of the subjective perceptions. This type, therefore, is uncommonly inaccessible to an

objective understanding and he fares no better in the understanding of himself.

Above all, his development estranges him from the reality of the object, handing him over to his subjective perceptions, which orientate his consciousness in accordance with an archaic reality, although his deficiency in comparative judgment keeps him wholly unaware of this fact. Actually he moves in a mythological world, where men animals, railways, houses, rivers, and mountains appear partly as benevolent deities and partly as malevolent demons. That thus they, appear to him never enters his mind, although their effect upon his judgments and acts can bear no other interpretation. He judges and acts as though he had such powers to deal with; but this begins to strike him only when he discovers that his sensations are totally different from reality. If his tendency is to reason objectively, he will sense this difference as morbid; but if, on the other hand, he remains faithful to his irrationality, and is prepared to grant his sensation reality value, the objective world will appear a mere make-belief and a comedy. Only in extreme cases, however, is this dilemma reached. As a rule, the individual acquiesces in his isolation and in the banality of the reality, which, however, he unconsciously treats archaically.

His unconscious is distinguished chiefly by the repression of intuition, which thereby acquires an extraverted and archaic character. Whereas true extraverted intuition has a characteristic resourcefulness, and a 'good nose' for every possibility in objective reality, this archaic, extraverted intuition has an amazing flair for every ambiguous, gloomy, dirty, and dangerous possibility in the background of reality. In the presence of this intuition the real and conscious intention of the object has no significance; it will peer behind every possible archaic antecedent of such an intention. It possesses, therefore, something dangerous, something actually undermining, which often stands in most vivid contrast to the gentle benevolence of consciousness. So long as the individual is not too aloof from the object, the unconscious intuition effects a wholesome compensation to the rather fantastic and over credulous attitude of consciousness. But as soon as the unconscious becomes antagonistic to consciousness, such intuitions come to the surface and expand their nefarious influence: they force themselves compellingly upon the individual, releasing compulsive ideas about objects of the most perverse kind. The neurosis arising from this sequence of events is usually a compulsion neurosis, in which the hysterical characters recede and are obscured by symptoms of exhaustion.

8. Intuition

Intuition, in the introverted attitude, is directed upon the inner object, a term we might justly apply to the elements of the unconscious. For the relation of inner objects to consciousness is entirely analogous to that of outer objects, although theirs is a psychological and not a physical reality. Inner objects appear to the intuitive perception as subjective images of things, which, though not met with in external experience, really determine the contents of the unconscious, i.e. the collective unconscious, in the last resort. Naturally, in their per se character, these contents are, not accessible to experience, a quality which they have in common with the outer object. For just as outer objects correspond only relatively with our perceptions of them, so the phenomenal forms of the inner object are also relative; products of their (to us) inaccessible essence and of the peculiar nature of the intuitive function. Like sensation, intuition also has its subjective factor, which is suppressed to the farthest limit in the extraverted intuition, but which becomes the decisive factor in the intuition of the introvert. Although this intuition may receive its impetus from outer objects, it is never arrested by the external possibilities, but stays with that factor which the outer object releases within.

Whereas introverted sensation is mainly confined to the perception of particular innervation phenomena by way of the unconscious, and does not go beyond them, intuition represses this side of the subjective factor and perceives the image which has really occasioned the innervation. Supposing, for instance, a man is overtaken by a psychogenic attack of giddiness. Sensation is arrested by the peculiar character of this innervationdisturbance, perceiving all its qualities, its intensity, its transient course, the nature of its origin and disappearance [p. 506] in their every detail, without raising the smallest inquiry concerning the nature of the thing which produced the disturbance, or advancing anything as to its content. Intuition, on the other hand, receives from the sensation only the impetus to immediate activity; it peers behind the scenes, quickly perceiving the inner image that gave rise to the specific phenomenon, *i.e.* the attack of vertigo, in the present case. It sees the image of a tottering man pierced through the heart by an arrow. This image fascinates the intuitive activity; it is arrested by it, and seeks to explore every detail of it. It holds fast to the vision, observing with the liveliest interest how the picture changes, unfolds further, and finally fades. In this way introverted intuition perceives all the background processes of consciousness with almost the same distinctness as extraverted sensation senses outer objects. For intuition, therefore, the unconscious images attain to the dignity of things or objects. But, because intuition excludes the co-operation of sensation, it obtains either no knowledge at all or at the best a very inadequate awareness of the innervation-disturbances or of the physical effects produced by the unconscious images. Accordingly, the images appear as though detached from the subject, as though existing in themselves without relation to the person.

Consequently, in the above-mentioned example, the introverted intuitive, when affected by the giddiness, would not imagine that the perceived image might also in some way refer to himself. Naturally, to one who is rationally orientated, such a thing seems almost unthinkable, but it is none the less a fact, and I have often experienced it in my dealings with this type.

The remarkable indifference of the extraverted intuitive in respect to outer objects is shared by the introverted intuitive in relation to the inner objects. Just as the extraverted intuitive is continually scenting out new possibilities, which he pursues with an equal unconcern both for his own welfare and for that of others, pressing on quite heedless of human considerations, tearing down what has only just been established in his everlasting search for change, so the introverted intuitive moves from image to image, chasing after every possibility in the teeming womb of the unconscious, without establishing any connection between the phenomenon and himself. Just as the world can never become a moral problem for the man who merely senses it, so the world of images is never a moral problem to the intuitive. To the one just as much as to the other, it is an *ae[]sthenic problem,* a question of perception, a 'sensation'. In this way, the consciousness of his own bodily existence fades from the introverted intuitive's view, as does its effect upon others. The extraverted standpoint would say of him: 'Reality has no existence for him; he gives himself up to fruitless phantasies'. A perception of the unconscious images, produced in such inexhaustible abundance by the creative energy of life, is of course fruitless from the standpoint of immediate utility. But, since these images represent possible ways of viewing life, which in given circumstances have the power to provide a new energic potential, this function, which to the outer world is the strangest of all, is as indispensable to the total psychic economy as is the corresponding human type to the psychic life of a people. Had this type not existed, there would have been no prophets in Israel.

Introverted intuition apprehends the images which arise from the a priori, *i.e.* the inherited foundations of the unconscious mind. These archetypes, whose innermost nature is inaccessible to experience, represent the precipitate of psychic functioning of the whole ancestral line, *i.e.* the heaped-up, or pooled, experiences of organic existence in general, a million times repeated, and condensed into types. Hence, in these archetypes all experiences are represented which since primeval time have happened on this planet. Their archetypal distinctness is the more marked, the more frequently and intensely they have been experienced. The archetype would be to borrow from Kant -- the noumenon of the image which intuition perceives and, in perceiving, creates.

Since the unconscious is not just something that lies there, like a psychic caput mortuum, but is something that coexists and experiences inner transformations which are inherently related to general events, introverted intuition, through its perception of inner processes, gives certain data which may possess supreme importance for the comprehension of general occurrences: it can even foresee new possibilities in more or less clear outline, as well as the event which later actually transpires. Its prophetic prevision is to be explained from its relation to the archetypes which represent the law-determined course of all experienceable things.

9. The Introverted Intuitive Type

The peculiar nature of introverted intuition, when given the priority, also produces a peculiar type of man, viz. the mystical dreamer and seer on the one hand, or the fantastical crank and artist on the other. The latter might be regarded as the normal case, since there is a general tendency of this type to confine himself to the perceptive character of intuition. As a rule, the intuitive stops at perception; perception is his principal problem, and -- in the case of a productive artist-the shaping of perception. But the crank contents himself with the intuition by which he himself is shaped and determined. Intensification of intuition naturally often results in an extraordinary aloofness of the individual from tangible reality; he may even become a complete enigma to his own immediate circle.

If an artist, he reveals extraordinary, remote things in his art, which in iridescent profusion embrace both the significant and the banal, the lovely and the grotesque, the whimsical and the sublime. If not an artist, he is frequently an unappreciated genius, a great man 'gone wrong', a sort of wise simpleton, a figure for 'psychological' novels.

Although it is not altogether in the line of the introverted intuitive type to make of perception a moral problem, since a certain reinforcement of the rational functions is required for this, yet even a relatively slight differentiation of judgment would suffice to transfer intuitive perception from the purely æsthetic into the moral sphere. A variety of this type is thus produced which differs essentially from its æsthetic form, although none the less characteristic of the introverted intuitive. The moral problem comes into being when the intuitive tries to relate himself to his vision, when he is no longer satisfied with mere perception and its æsthetic shaping and estimation, but confronts the question: What does this mean for me and for the world? What emerges from this vision in the way of a duty or task, either for me or for the world? The pure intuitive who represses judgment or possesses it only under the spell of perception never meets this question fundamentally, since his only problem is the How of perception. He, therefore, finds the moral problem unintelligible, even absurd, and as far as possible forbids his thoughts to dwell upon the disconcerting vision. It is different with the morally orientated intuitive. He concerns himself with the meaning of his vision; he troubles less about its further æsthetic possibilities than about the possible moral effects which emerge from its intrinsic significance.

His judgment allows him to discern, though often only darkly, that he, as a man and as a totality, is in some way inter-related with his vision, that it is something which cannot just be perceived but which also would fain become the life of the subject. Through this realization he feels bound to transform his vision into his own life. But, since he tends to rely exclusively upon his vision, his moral effort becomes one-sided; he makes himself and his life symbolic, adapted, it is true, to the inner and eternal meaning of events, but unadapted to the actual present-day reality. Therewith he also deprives himself of any influence upon it, because he remains unintelligible. His language is not that which is commonly spoken -- it becomes too subjective. His argument lacks convincing reason. He can only confess or pronounce. His is the 'voice of one crying in the wilderness'.

The introverted intuitive's chief repression falls upon the sensation of the object. His unconscious is characterized by this fact. For we find in his unconscious a compensatory extraverted sensation function of an archaic character. The unconscious personality may, therefore, best be described as an extraverted sensation-type of a rather low and primitive order. Impulsiveness and unrestraint are the characters of this sensation, combined with an extraordinary dependence upon the sense impression. This latter quality is a compensation to the thin upper air of the conscious attitude, giving it a certain weight, so that complete 'sublimation' is prevented. But if, through a forced exaggeration of the conscious attitude, a complete subordination to the inner perception should develop, the unconscious becomes an opposition, giving rise to compulsive sensations whose excessive dependence upon the object is in frank conflict with the conscious attitude. The form of neurosis is a compulsion-neurosis, exhibiting symptoms that are partly hypochondriacal manifestations, partly hypersensibility of the sense organs and partly compulsive ties to definite persons or other objects.

10. Recapitulation of Introverted Irrational Types

The two types just depicted are almost inaccessible to external judgment. Because they are introverted and have in consequence a somewhat meagre capacity or willingness for expression, they offer but a frail handle for a telling criticism. Since their main activity is directed within, nothing is outwardly visible but reserve, secretiveness, lack of sympathy, or uncertainty, and an apparently groundless perplexity. When anything does come to the surface, it usually consists in indirect manifestations of inferior and relatively unconscious functions. Manifestations of such a nature naturally excite a certain environmental prejudice against these types.

Accordingly they are mostly underestimated, or at least misunderstood. To the same degree as they fail to understand themselves -- because they very largely lack judgment -- they are also powerless to understand why they are so constantly undervalued by public opinion. They cannot see that their outward-going expression is, as a matter of fact, also of an inferior character. Their vision is enchanted by the abundance of subjective events. What happens there is so captivating, and of such inexhaustible attraction, that they do not appreciate the fact that their habitual communications to their circle express very, little of that real experience in which they themselves are, as it were, caught up. The fragmentary and, as a rule, quite episodic character of their communications make too great a demand upon the understanding and good will of their circle; furthermore, their mode of expression lacks that flowing warmth to the object which alone can have convincing force. On the contrary, these types show very often a brusque, repelling demeanour towards the outer world, although of this they are quite unaware, and have not the least intention of showing it. We shall form a [p. 512] fairer judgment of such men and grant them a greater indulgence, when we begin to realize how hard it is to translate into intelligible language what is perceived within. Yet this indulgence must not be so liberal as to exempt them altogether from the necessity of such expression. This could be only detrimental for such types. Fate itself prepares for them, perhaps even more than for other men, overwhelming external difficulties, which have a very sobering effect upon the intoxication of the inner vision. But frequently only an intense personal need can wring from them a human expression.

From an extraverted and rationalistic standpoint, such types are indeed the most fruitless of men. But, viewed from a higher standpoint, such men are living evidence of the fact that this rich and varied world with its overflowing and intoxicating life is not purely external, but also exists within. These types are admittedly one sided demonstrations of Nature, but they are an educational experience for the man who refuses to be blinded by the intellectual mode of the day. In their own way, men with such an attitude are educators and promoters of culture. Their life teaches more than their words. From their lives, and not the least from what is just their greatest fault, viz. their incommunicability, we may understand one of the greatest errors of our civilization, that is, the superstitious belief in statement and presentation, the immoderate overprizing of instruction by means of word and method. A child certainly allows himself to be impressed by the grand talk of its parents. But is it really imagined that the child is thereby educated? Actually it is the parents' lives that educate the child -- what they add thereto by word and gesture at best serves only to confuse him. The same holds good for the teacher. But we have such a belief in method that, if only the method be good, the practice of it seems to hallow the teacher. An inferior [p. 513] man is never. a good teacher. But he can conceal his injurious inferiority, which secretly poisons the pupil, behind an excellent method or, an equally brilliant intellectual capacity. Naturally the pupil of riper years desires nothing better than the knowledge of useful methods, because he is already defeated by the general attitude, which believes in the victorious method. He has already learnt that the emptiest head, correctly echoing a method, is the best pupil. His whole environment not only urges but exemplifies the doctrine that all success and happiness are external, and that only the right method is needed to attain the haven of one's desires. Or is the life of his religious instructor likely to demonstrate that happiness which radiates from the treasure of the inner vision? The irrational introverted types are certainly no instructors of a more complete humanity. They lack reason and the ethics of reason, but their lives teach the other possibility, in which our civilization is so deplorably wanting.

11. The Principal and Auxiliary Functions

In the foregoing descriptions I have no desire to give my readers the impression that such pure types occur at all frequently in actual practice. The are, as it were, only Galtonesque familyportraits, which sum up in a cumulative image the common and therefore typical characters, stressing these disproportionately, while the individual features are just as disproportionately effaced. Accurate investigation of the individual case consistently reveals the fact that, in conjunction with the most differentiated function, another function of secondary importance, and therefore of inferior differentiation in consciousness, is constantly present, and is a -- relatively determining factor.

For the sake of clarity let us again recapitulate: The products of all the functions can be conscious, but we speak of the consciousness of a function only when not merely its application is at the disposal of the will, but when at the same time its principle is decisive for the orientation of consciousness. The latter event is true when, for instance, thinking is not a mere esprit de l'escalier, or rumination, but when its decisions possess an absolute validity, so that the logical conclusion in a given case holds good, whether as motive or as guarantee of practical action, without the backing of any further evidence. This absolute sovereignty always belongs, empirically, to one function alone, and *can* belong only to one function, since the equally independent intervention of another function would necessarily yield a different orientation, which would at least partially contradict the first. But, since it is a vital condition for the conscious adaptation-process that constantly clear and unambiguous aims should be in evidence, the presence of a second function of equivalent power is naturally forbidden' This other function, therefore, can have only a secondary importance, a fact which is also established empirically. Its secondary importance consists in the fact that, in a given case, it is not valid in its own right, as is the primary function, as an absolutely reliable and decisive factor, but comes into play more as an auxiliary or complementary function. Naturally only those functions can appear as auxiliary whose nature is not opposed to the leading function. For instance, feeling can never act as the second function by the side of thinking, because its nature stands in too strong a contrast to thinking. Thinking, if it is to be real thinking and true to its own principle, must scrupulously exclude feeling. This, of course, does not exclude the fact that individuals certainly exist in whom thinking and feeling stand upon the same [p. level, whereby both have equal motive power in con~sdousness. But, in such a case, there is also no question of a differentiated type, but merely of a relatively undeveloped thinking and feeling. Uniform consciousness and unconsciousness of functions is, therefore, a distinguishing mark of a primitive mentality.

Experience shows that the secondary function is always one whose nature is different from, though not antagonistic to, the leading function : thus, for example, thinking, as primary function, can readily pair with intuition as auxiliary, or indeed equally well with sensation, but, as already observed, never with feeling. Neither intuition nor sensation are antagonistic to thinking, *i.e.* they have not to be unconditionally excluded, since they are not, like feeling, of similar nature, though of opposite purpose, to thinking -- for as a judging function feeling successfully competes with thinking -- but are functions of perception, affording welcome assistance to thought. As soon as they reached the same level of differentiation as thinking, they would cause a change of attitude, which would contradict the tendency of thinking. For they would convert the judging attitude into a perceiving one; whereupon the principle of rationality indispensable to thought would be suppressed in favour of the irrationality of mere perception. Hence the auxiliary function is possible and useful only in so far as it *serves* the leading function, without making any claim to the autonomy of its own principle.

For all the types appearing in practice, the principle holds good that besides the conscious main function there is also a relatively unconscious, auxiliary function which is in every respect different from the nature of the main function. From these combinations well-known pictures arise, the practical intellect for instance paired with sensation, the speculative intellect breaking through [p. 516] with intuition, the artistic intuition which selects. and presents its images by means of feeling judgment, the philosophical intuition which, in league with a vigorous intellect, translates its vision into the sphere of comprehensible thought, and so forth.

A grouping of the unconscious functions also takes place in accordance with the relationship of the conscious functions. Thus, for instance, an unconscious intuitive feeling attitude may correspond with a conscious practical intellect, whereby the function of feeling suffers a relatively stronger inhibition than intuition. This peculiarity, however, is of interest only for one who is concerned with the practical psychological treatment of such cases. But for such a man it is important to know about it. For I have frequently observed the way in which a physician, in the case for instance of an exclusively intellectual subject, will do his utmost to develop the feeling function directly out of the unconscious. This attempt must always come to grief, since it involves too great a violation of the conscious standpoint. Should such a violation succeed, there ensues a really compulsive dependence of the patient upon the physician, a 'transference' which can be amputated only by brutality, because such a violation robs the patient of a standpoint -

- his physician becomes his standpoint. But the approach to the unconscious and to the most repressed function is disclosed, as it were, of itself, and with more adequate protection of the conscious standpoint, when the way of development is *via* the secondary function-thus in the case of a rational type by way of the irrational function. For this lends the conscious standpoint such a range and prospect over what is possible and imminent that consciousness gains an adequate protection against the destructive effect of the unconscious. Conversely, an irrational type demands a stronger development of the rational auxiliary function represented in consciousness, in order to be sufficiently prepared to receive the impact of the unconscious.

The unconscious functions are in an archaic, animal state. Their symbolical appearances in dreams and phantasies usually represent the battle or coming encounter of two animals or monsters.